S M A R T
G R O W T H

A Prescription for

SMART Growth

for Small to Mid-Size Businesses

1	2	3	4	5			6	7	8	9	10	11
St	Ma	Al	RO	Te			Go	Re	OE	WC	Tr	HG
12	13	14	15	16	17	18	19	20	21	22	23	24
Ac	Ao	CF	CA	CS	Em	Le	Li	Me	Pe	Pr	Qu	Rl
25	26		27	28	29	30	31	32	33	34	35	36
Rs	Re		Ca	Ge	In	Uf	Ov	Pj	Ps	Rs	Sr	Ty

Jack Spain

www.SMARTGrowthSMB.com

A Prescription for **SMART** Growth for Small to Mid-Size Businesses

Publisher: **Spain T**echnovative **Solutions**
Cover Design: Chris Duke, The WYSIWYG Group
                http://www.TheWYSIWYGGroup.com

Printed in the United States of America

1st Edition – January 2013

    ISBN 978-0-615-71110-2
    1. Smart Growth. 2. Business Growth. 3. Business Leadership.
    4. Management. 5. Business Strategy. 6. Small and Mid-Size
    Businesses. 7. Business Coaching. 8. Business Symptoms.
    9. Business Diagnosis. 10. Business Prescriptions.

This book is dedicated to my brother Michael whose spirit continues to inspire and motivate me every day from his creativity, compassion, interest, introspect and empathy for everything that he encountered.

Jack Spain
Spain Business Advisors
Cary, NC USA
jack <at> SMARTGrowthSMB.com
http://www.SMARTGrowthSMB.com
http://www.jackspain.com

Table of Contents

Forward

I first met Jack Spain during the rollercoaster ride of the dotcom boom that began in the late 1990's. I had built up a resume that included a couple of failed startups along with a range of experiences in large Fortune 500 companies and small businesses, centered mostly around technology – specifically local area networks, implementation management, software development, and personal computing support.

By the time Jack brought me onboard at SciQuest, the pre-IPO company was moving like a locomotive heading into open territory, laying track just ahead of the engine car as it sped along. SciQuest picked up speed and grew quickly from 150 or so people when I started in 1999, to 450+. Then, the bubble popped, the train lost steam, losing money fell out of fashion, and the company was forced to dramatically reduce the passenger count. Jack left in 2001 and I hung on until 2003 when it was time to step off voluntarily and try something else. It was a great thrill ride with no shortage of opportunities to acquire a wealth of knowledge about how businesses should, and should not, grow.

Jack went on to fill executive roles at other companies, then worked as a consultant in his own businesses, helping executives and business owners pursue their growth and development goals. In each role, Jack focused on his core skills – research, organization, leadership, and execution.

I chose a slightly different path, growing a small business that my wife and I started in late 2001. Anna's Gourmet Goodies is a successful online retailer of hand-made, gourmet cookie gifts, shipping orders throughout the US and military bases around the world. It is a business that has grown organically out of passion for excellence and a desire to create a profitable, debt-free, sustainable business.

I've since helped start, operate and grow another Internet-based company into a solid, profitable enterprise, starting with virtually no capital and relying on a virtual infrastructure. I have a few more ideas still inside the oven that may emerge at the appropriate time in the future, all based on the concept of growing businesses that actually support themselves and are profitable.

Jack and I have shared many conversations over the years about our experiences and what it takes to not only start, but grow a business. Growth, not just by throwing resources (money, time, human capital) at an idea or a problem, but by combining the passion required for success with sound principles for developing the business in a way that is sustainable and uses resources efficiently.

Two key elements that broadly encompass Jack's approach to business growth and this book are:

1. Avoiding unnecessary mistakes by learning from what others have done well, and poorly.

2. Asking questions and digesting the answers, no matter how unpleasant they may be sometimes, to develop the skill of continuous improvement that comes by embracing wisdom from other successful people.

Does that mean that if you answer all the questions in this book you will not fail? Absolutely not. Failure is a critical component of success.

Jack's belief is that smart growth is born out of a passion to move forward in the most efficient manner possible by asking questions and paying attention to the answers. Making the same mistakes over and over again and expecting different results is not smart; it's the definition of insanity.

Smart growth is not about having all the correct answers to every question, but rather about a framework for asking questions, developing answers, executing plans, and repeating the process. Not every question in this book applies to every business. Collectively, they provide a working model to implement sound business principles and move your business forward.

At first glance, you might be overwhelmed thinking that you need to have the answer for every question as soon as possible. Successful people, entrepreneurs, and executives understand that business is a marathon, not a sprint. Just keep putting one foot in front of the other – one step at a time.

Practicing smart growth strategies, instead of burning all your fuel in the first few seconds of a race, will increase the odds you'll make it to the finish line instead of ending up prematurely in the graveyard of great ideas. I see this book as a framework to help you either get started or re-align yourself along a path towards smart growth in your business.

What do you see?

Chris Duke
Husband. Father. Technologist. Entrepreneur.
http://www.ChrisDuke.com

Preface

"Toto, I've a feeling we're not in Kansas any more."
– Dorothy, from the *"Wizard of Oz"*

Small businesses are the engine that powers the economy in the United States and throughout the world. While the media tends to focus a great deal of attention on large corporations, small businesses are working feverishly to drive innovation and create new products, services, and exciting career opportunities for many of us. According to the US Small Business Administration[1]:

- Small businesses represent 99.7% of all employer firms
- Small businesses employ half of the US private sector employees
- Small businesses create more than 50% of the nonfarm private gross domestic product (GDP)
- Small businesses have generated 65% of the new jobs over the past almost two decades
- Small businesses produce 13 to 14 times more patents per employee than their larger counterparts
- There are almost 23 million small businesses throughout the US

During the past four decades I have had the distinct pleasure to meet, support, and collaborate with hundreds of small and mid-size business owners. Many of these entrepreneurs did not intentionally set out to fulfill a long-term dream and many have not written a formal strategic business plan. Many

---

[1] www.sba.gov

Preface

entrepreneurs were able to successfully launch a new business at the right time and the right place with the right idea. While some may attribute their success to wisdom and insight; many will admit that they had some good luck along the way. Despite their beginnings, a common thread of all successful business owners is sacrifice, commitment, and hard work.

Not surprising though, many entrepreneurs suddenly wake up and realize that they now have 25, 50, 100, 250, or maybe even 500 associates that now depend on them to continue to lead a successful business enterprise. What occurs more often than not is that your internal "systems" are no longer practical, effective, and most likely efficient to run the business. By "systems" I am referring to internal processes, procedures, and infrastructure including the technology and business software applications. You may also have recently observed that you may not have the necessary skills and experiences on-board to get your business to the next level, whatever those requirements may be.

Entrepreneurs interested in growing a business must hone skills to recognize the **symptoms**; **diagnose** the problem; and identify the right **prescriptions** to move the business in a positive direction. The challenge that many business leaders face today is how do you identify the challenges and implement the required adjustments considering (1) you do not have the time as your business may already be moving at the speed of light and has fully consumed you; (2) your business depends on you a great deal to survive on a day-to-day basis; and (3) you do not personally have the experience and insights to identify and implement the changes required to stabilize your operation and position your business for the next stage of growth.

Virtually everyone's story is different regarding the genesis of their business and the adventures, successes, trials, and tribulations experienced to date. Quite often though there is a common chapter in most business' history where the founder or current business leader experiences their *"**Whoa...; how did I get here?**"* moment that includes questions like the following:

- How did I get here?
- Why did this happen?
- What do I do about it?
- Where do I go from here?
- When is it going to get better?
- How Much effort is this going to take?

This book was born out of a passion to answer these and many other questions that keep small to mid-size business leaders awake a night. Through my interactions with various business owners I have found that it can be *very lonely at the top*, as business leaders of small to mid-size businesses quite often do not have a *"sounding board"*, or team of trusted subordinates and advisors to discuss and debate executive-level decisions and provide candid and objective feedback.

My objective was to provide business leaders with a synergistic framework to recognize **symptoms** indicating potential dysfunction in your business; **diagnose** the problems; and recommend proven **prescriptions** to address challenges that inhibit growth. The reader will find hundreds of questions, reflections, guidance, and specific action items to put you firmly in control of your destiny and prepare you to pursue your dreams, however tactical or far-reaching they may be. Please note that the questions included throughout this book are not intended to threaten, intimidate, or discourage business leaders. My goal was to potentially

Preface

challenge your current thinking, become a catalyst for growing your business, and inspire you to identify and implement innovative and novel solutions and approaches to grow your business in a logical, sustainable fashion.

Introduction

"Customer satisfaction, Employee satisfaction and Cash flow are the three most important indicators for a business." — Jack Welch

Whether you are leading a business-to-consumer (B2C) or business-to-business (B2B) company, the most significant challenges that all small and mid-size business (**SMB**) leaders face today are typically:

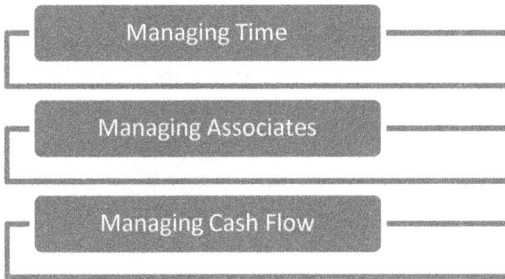

Managing Time

Managing Associates

Managing Cash Flow

Time is quite often your most critical resource and of course there is never enough of it. As your business' leader *(founder, owner, president, chief executive, managing partner, etc.)*, it is essential that you take the responsibility to continuously prioritize your time to focus on obtaining the highest return on investment from your vision, knowledge, experience, insights, instincts, and passion for your business. Quite often you represent the ***brains*** and ***central nervous system*** for your business and must make certain that you are getting optimal utilization of the precious time you have available.

It is also crucial for you to effectively manage and maximize the return on investment from each of your **associates** *(staff, team members, employees, etc.)* that are assisting you in supporting your clients in the delivery of products, services,

Introduction

and solutions for your business. Your associates are the *muscle* that you exercise to power and strengthen your business on a daily basis – and it is vitally important that they remain in top condition to delivery optimal performance each and every day.

Simultaneously, you must also always keep your eye on your business results (i.e. financials), including your ability to maintain sufficient cash reserves to support your day-to-day tactical requirements as well as your long-term strategic objectives. I view your business' **cash flow** as the fuel that delivers *nutrition* to feed your specific business requirements on a daily basis as well as a gauge of the *overall health* of your business. To improve your cash flow, you can simply increase revenues *(sell more things)* and/or reduce your costs *(improve margins and/or reduce fixed costs)*. While it is a simple equation to describe, it is often quite challenging to deliver on a consistent basis without tremendous discipline, implementing the key elements described in the **SMART Growth** model, and of course, a little luck.

Most business owners I meet with on a regular basis are not satisfied with their current results and aspire to position their business to attract and capture additional revenues from established as well as new prospective clients. As a business leader, do you take the time to reflect on whether you are doing the *right things* the *right way* across your business to attract and secure additional business opportunities? How would you respond to the following questions relative to your current position to scale your business?

- Have you identified specific changes that you can make internally to position your business to capture additional market share?

- Have you prioritized your target prospects and new market opportunities recently?

- Do you have the right associates in place today to support scaling your business revenues by 10x?

- Have you determined which investments in people, process, technology, and infrastructure that would deliver the maximum return for your business relative to positioning your business for new growth opportunities?

- Have you conducted research to reveal if any recent innovations may have a fundamental impact on how you efficiently design, develop, deliver, service, and support your current portfolio of products and services?

Of course, timing is an extremely important factor if you are contemplating growing your business. Growth requires focus, resources, determination, tremendous effort, and a roadmap. Here are a few additional questions to determine if the timing is right for you.

- Would you consider your business to be in a chaos mode – or are you positioned to focus simultaneously on your day-to-day business execution requirements in conjunction with your longer-term goals?

- Can your team address new challenges without your day-to-day oversight, guidance, and support?

Introduction

- Have you conceived and documented a plan with specific goals and milestones to grow your business during the next three to five years?

In order to be in a position to scale your business, you must be firmly established to lead your business. Unless you are born lucky, and sometimes good fortune in the form of new clients and large orders drop in our lap; you must have the time to think strategically, design and implement key changes to your business, train your associates, and oversee your efforts to successfully execute at a greater rate than you have experienced in the past *(highly abbreviated description)*.

One method to evaluate if the timing is right for you is to determine if you are currently a *"servant"* of your business; currently focused on *"managing"* your business; or whether you are fortunate to have attained a state where you are *"leading"* your business. Many SMB leaders navigate from state to state much like negotiating your way down a whitewater river which demands different responses as you traverse from still water to Class 2 through Class 4 rapids and back to still water again. Successful business leaders learn to read and interpret the signs ahead and anticipate the response and leadership style required for each situation. The following table provides several insights to determine what role you are currently serving in your business.

Servant	Managing	Leading
I am in a constant daily firefight for survival	I am able to delegate non-critical issues and tasks to my associates	I am able to define and manage my priorities the majority of the time
It is impossible to plan my day, let alone tomorrow or the week ahead	I set goals each week and am able to get to maybe ½ of them in a good week	I am successful more often than not in meeting the daily, weekly, monthly, and quarterly goals that I have established for myself

Servant	Managing	Leading
I am too busy and have no time to prioritize all the things that I have to deal with every day	I prioritize my key tasks weekly, but many times our daily crises prevent me from getting to my to-do list	I subscribe to Brian Tracy's *"Eat That Frog!"*[2] method to avoid procrastination and attempt to remain focused and productive each day
There is a constant line of associates outside the revolving door to my office	I have regularly scheduled meetings, but still have to deal with interruptions on a frequent basis	I have scheduled weekly, monthly, and annual meetings in advance to address both tactical and strategic topics on a timely basis
We typically react and create an ad-hoc response to each new challenges and request	My associates are fairly adept at handling many of our unforeseen issues and challenges	We have documented processes and procedures and effective on-going training for our associates
We create agendas on-the-fly as issues and tasks come to our attention	We develop an agenda for our meetings at the beginning of each formal meeting	We require an agenda before each meeting which all associates are expected to review and be prepared in advance of our meetings
We pull different associates together as needed for discussions and planning	We use email to announce meeting times and locations	We have an electronic calendar that all associates have access to for scheduling meetings
We invest time as required to support the needs of our clients and business	We do our best to keep meetings on topic and to not wander too far from our agenda	Our team members have respect for each associate's time and use it prudently

The recommendations presented throughout this book provide you with guidelines to position you and your business associates to be more productive in order for you to achieve your professional and personal goals and aspirations. As time is one of our most precious resources, one objective I had in developing this book was not to ramble and digress for hundreds of pages, elaborating on each and every

---

[2] http://www.briantracy.com/catalog/product.aspx?pid=465

Introduction

recommendation and action item that I have incorporated into this publication. My aim was to be concise and position this book as a valuable reference tool to use for reflection by business leaders who are interested and committed to growing their business. I clearly recognize that SMB leaders do not have the time to read a 300-400 page textbook in fine print and my goal was not to publish yet another book that would never leave its position in the bookshelf.

The prescriptions that I offer will certainly not provide you with all the answers for each and every one of your current and future challenges, but I firmly believe that it will provide you with many valuable questions to reflect upon along with a related set of specific actions to assist you in maximizing you business' growth potential. I will caution you in advance that if you are currently satisfied with your successes achieved to-date, your market penetration, and your current growth trajectory; that I anticipate that you may not be interested in investing the required energy, effort, and perspiration to implement the recommendations for your business that I have highlighted throughout this book. My prescriptions will also likely not be too relevant if you happen to be in a position where you are *"fighting for your life"* to remain in business. On the other hand, I certainly do hope that you embrace and implement the recommendations that I have shared to position you to lead your business to wherever levels you aspire to take it.

Why Grow Your Business?

"Without continual growth and progress, such words as improvement, achievement, and success have no meaning." – Benjamin Franklin
"Growth is the oxygen of business, the key to business life or death. Growing enterprises thrive; shrinking companies vanish."
– Michael Treacy

A good place to start is to elaborate on why it is important to proactively plan to grow your business in the first place. What's in it for you as an already overwhelmed and overworked business leader? You are likely already facing more challenges then you believe you can deal with most days and it is showing no signs of slowing down. Included below is some *"food for thought"* to provide a frame of reference on why it is imperative that you commit to a plan and a process to grow your business.

1. Clients continue to have higher expectations and demand more from their product and service providers each and every day.

2. Despite what you do and how you are doing it, another business would love to have your clients – especially their cash.

3. Regardless of what degree we are wired to resist change – change is constant, and the rate of change continues to accelerate.

4. Growing your business is a very effective method to reward your associates with new challenges, experiences, and career options – and a very positive means to minimize staff turnover.

5. Many business leaders have a need to feed their entrepreneurial spirit which was formulated in their DNA at conception, as well as providing you with the opportunity to *"fulfill the American Dream"* that many of us have aspired for a long time.

6. As your specific requirements to support and supply your clients' increases, so does your negotiating leverage with your suppliers and business partners.

7. Scaling your business often has a very positive impact on your local and regional ecosystems.

8. Growing your business delivers financial rewards for you and your family, as well as potential rewarding career opportunities for multiple generations.

9. Increasing your business generates returns that you can donate to your favorite charitable organizations.

10. Expanding your business presents you with an opportunity to leave a legacy that your family and community can appreciate for generations.

With this context, I will introduce a "**SMART**" approach to successfully grow your business in a fashion where you, your associates, and your clients will succeed.

Overview of the **SMART** Growth Model

"A man must be big enough to admit his mistakes, smart enough to profit from them, and strong enough to correct them."
— John C. Maxwell

The following model incorporates underlying characteristics of businesses that have been successful in emerging from their start-up phase into a sustained growth stage. This model is based on my experience working with a variety of businesses of different shapes and sizes across diverse industries over the past several decades. While each and every business is unique with their own distinctive set of challenges and opportunities, I have discovered that these universal and fundamental characteristics of successful growth businesses that include a concentration on being:

- **S**trategy-based
- **M**arket-based
- **A**lignment-based
- **R**OI-based
- **T**echnology-based

While many authors attempt to design an overly simple, straight-forward, magic formula or basic set of guidelines to lead a business; my experience has taught me that running a successful business is a complex proposition. The job becomes even more challenging when your mission includes leading your business on a continuous growth trajectory. I have come to realize that in conjunction with the key business characteristics highlighted above, there are a number of additional success attributes or building blocks which also merit the attention and an appropriate priority of the respective business leaders *(not necessarily in this sequence)*:

1. *Emphasis on* **accountability**
2. *Emphasis on* **action-orientation**
3. *Emphasis on* **cash flow**
4. *Emphasis on* **client acquisition**
5. *Emphasis on* **client service**
6. *Emphasis on* **empowerment**
7. *Emphasis on* **leadership**
8. *Emphasis on* **listening**
9. *Emphasis on* **metrics**
10. *Emphasis on* **perseverance**
11. *Emphasis on* **prioritization**
12. *Emphasis on* **quality**
13. *Emphasis on* **relationships**
14. *Emphasis on* **results**
15. *Emphasis on* **root cause analysis**

While formalities like organization structure, policies, and procedures are necessary to some degree for any successful business including SMBs, it is imperative that you do not place too much focus on certain aspects of growing your business that could ultimately impede and stall growth. Based on my experience, I also recommend that leaders implement:

1. *Just enough* **communication**
2. *Just enough* **governance**
3. *Just enough* **information**
4. *Just enough* **infrastructure**
5. *Just enough* **oversight**
6. *Just enough* **planning**
7. *Just enough* **process**
8. *Just enough* **resources**
9. *Just enough* **structure**

10. *Just enough* **technology**

The following chapters provide more details on these characteristics and attributes and provide the reader with a series of questions to ponder along with a set of specific actions to place your business on a successful and efficient growth trajectory.

Creating a Strategy-based Culture

"In the business world, the rearview mirror is always clearer than the windshield." – Warren Buffett
"... those who look only to the past or present are certain to miss the future." – John F. Kennedy
"Plans are useless, but planning is indispensable."
– Dwight D. Eisenhower

It is imperative for business leaders to formulate an overarching vision supported by a strategy that incorporates where you want to go; how long it will take; and how you will get there – to name a few critical elements. A successful company is established with a shared sense of direction – a roadmap – a game plan to communicate, educate, illuminate, guide, and inspire your team. Your strategy should define how you plan to achieve the vision and mission that inspired the founder(s) to launch the business. It should also serve to guide you to make prudent decisions on acquiring and allocating the required resources to operate your business.

A business strategy should be supported by specific *goals* or *objectives* on what you must accomplish to achieve your strategy. I am a fan of Jim Collins' **BHAG**[3] *(Big Hairy Audacious Goal)* concept. Your goals should ultimately inspire your associates to work collaboratively to accomplish things that few could envision and even fewer could imagine that they could achieve. Business leaders must be cautious though not to set goals so far-reaching that it ultimately results in discouraging your associates. The specific goals will vary

---

[3] http://www.jimcollins.com/media_topics/building-greatness.html

dramatically from business to business. Examples of goals that may be applicable to your business include:

- Achieving the top 20% in our market for industry customer service ratings
- Targeting a 25% increase in revenue during this calendar year
- Achieving a 5% improvement in our gross margin for our most recent product line
- Striving for a 10x improvement in our monthly cash flow within 24 months
- Realizing a 2x product inventory turns improvement by the end of the fiscal year
- Decreasing our receivables balance by 15% within 90 days.
- Increasing staff productivity by 25%
- Successfully launching three new revenue streams within the next 18 months
- Decreasing current liabilities (credit card balances) by 50% during the next 12 months
- Realizing a more reasonable work-life balance by the beginning of summer
- Implementing the next major systems upgrade within the next 6 months

As in driving a vehicle, it is dangerous to lead your business by focusing your attention on the rearview mirror. SMB leaders must be looking forward, anticipating, planning, and responding to the road ahead and oncoming traffic. While analyzing historical results is essential to gauging whether you are on course, a leader must continue to focus on what is ahead.

Creating a Strategy-based Culture

Symptoms of Potential **S**trategy-based Challenges

I have included several questions that may expose symptoms of potential strategy-related challenges within your business.

- When was the last time you were in a position to pause and revisit your business strategy with respect to the current market dynamics and competitive landscape?

- Has your business been consistently meeting, exceeding, or falling short of your growth expectations?

- Are your current innovation and improvement initiatives positioning you as a leader, a fast follower, or are you beginning to fall behind?

- Are you or one of your associates investing time to conduct market research on a regular basis?

- Are you facing a crossroads where you are starting to contemplate introducing a paradigm shift to redirect your business in a new direction?

Diagnostic Questions for Potential **S**trategy Challenges

To determine pertinent diagnosis options to potential growth strategy challenges, a good place to start is to spend a few minutes reflecting on your responses to the following questions:

1. **Who** are your target clients and in what industries and markets?

2. **What** are the core products and services that you offer, or are planning to offer in the near term?

3. **When** is the ideal time to introduce new products and services from your current product roadmap your clients?

4. **Where** are you planning to market your products and services? Are you sure this is the optimal delivery vehicle and/or media for your target markets? Do you have data or results supporting your approach?

5. **Why** would a prospective buyer acquire products and services from your business versus a competitor (i.e. what is your organization's strategic competitive advantage over competing offerings for products and services)?

6. **How** are you planning to deliver your products and services to your customers?

7. **How Much** are you willing to invest in your next generation products and services and how much risk are you willing to accept?

8. **How** do you know that your responses and perceptions to these questions are "reality-based", or are you potentially operating in isolation from the marketplace and clients that you are serving?

9. **What** threats in the form of new products or services that may emerge in the next 18 months that could potentially put you out of business?

10. **How Much** of your current strategic planning is triggered by a reaction to a challenging event, or have you instituted a process to periodically update, validate, and realign your business's strategy?

Prescriptions for **SMART** Growth

I recommend that business leaders consider the following actions to build a **S**trategy-based culture.

1. Ensure that you have **access to key market** and **industry data** to keep you and your team grounded in the realities versus perceptions about your target market. Your own professional network can be extremely beneficial on this front along with the contacts that you meet at industry conferences, seminars, and meetings. Effective strategic planning begins with research, information, insights, and instincts into what is ahead.

2. Take the time periodically to revisit those critical elements that provide your business with a **strategic competitive advantage**. Do you have a good understanding of what has changed both internally and externally to your business since the last time you updated your plan? Has your organization lost focus and intensity recently – or have you been potentially focusing on the wrong elements of your business? Are you

currently on target to meet your goals, or does your business need some course corrections?

3. Reassess your vision and current **expectations for growth** for your next planning period. Do your growth expectations really challenge your business or can you accomplish them by remaining on auto-pilot? Do you have the financial, personnel, and infrastructure resources in place to achieve your goals? What new innovations will be required in order for you to achieve your goals? Do you have sufficient resources and the right resources to get you there?

4. Institute a **process for strategic planning**. This does not have to be a rigid, time-consuming, *"stop everything until it is completed"* process – but you should establish a timeframe *(one year or less)* in which you pause long enough to consciously revisit your business strategy on a recurring basis *(ideally during a time of the year where your business is not running at its peak)*. What are your successes? What are your shortfalls? Can you identify the root causes behind your misses? What do you need to do differently? What has changed since the last planning period? Are you competitors standing still or gaining ground in your market? What new players have emerged that you need to follow closely?

   After time for reflection – your plan should be realigned, refocused, documented, communicated, and implemented supported by a detailed action plan with responsibilities and dates. Ideally, you should strive to institute an *evergreen process* that continues to invigorate your business on a regular basis and preserve your long-term viability in your target markets.

5. Take the time to update and **document your strategic plan** for your business. It certainly does not have to be voluminous, but it is important to identify and acknowledge your challenges, opportunities, vision, goals, and objectives. It does not really matter if your plan is one page or twenty pages as long as you have invested the time to validate and update your plan. I find that you receive far more value from the soul-searching, reflection, research, analysis and collaboration which are key elements of this process then you receive from a formal document that you will likely file away in an electronic or paper folder until it is time to pause again.

   In other words, it has been my experience that you ultimately derive greater benefit from the *strategic planning process* than from the final document you produce. There are numerous templates available from a quick Internet search if you are unsure where to start. After you have launched your business you must be **pragmatic** relative to reviewing and updating your plan. Please keep in mind that you can often invest 20% of the effort in this endeavor to achieve 80% of the value from your strategic planning process *(80/20 Rule)*.

6. Business leaders should continue to **validate your strategies** and make adjustments as necessary while being conscientious not to create too much disruption, too fast across your organization. Validation comes through business results, customer feedback, and being cognizant of changes in your marketplace. This is where previous experience leading change management initiatives can be a tremendous asset for your business.

7. When identifying and establishing goals for your organization, follow the guidelines provided by experts for decades to create **SMART goals** (Specific,

<u>M</u>easurable, <u>A</u>ttainable, <u>R</u>ealistic, *and* <u>T</u>imely)[4] [5]. Your goals should be the fuel to motivate, energize, and guide your associates. As the business leader it is imperative to verify that your goals are synergistic and that do not inadvertently result in conflicting priorities across your business. This can result in the antithesis of alignment that we discuss in a later chapter. Investing the time to identify clear goals is one of the most objective tools that you can implement to measure progress and success across your business, beyond a set of monthly or quarterly financial statements.

8. Establish specific **individual goals** for each of your team members *(refer to SMART goals above)* that will help ensure that you are successful in meeting the overarching goals for your business. Ideally, each individual goal for your associates should directly support your business goals. As your organization get larger, this will be more challenging and you will find that some associates will have specific goals that indirectly support your overall business goals.

   You should verify that you goals meet a number of acid tests, including are your goals reality-based and achievable? Have you set the goals high enough to inspire extraordinary performance without crossing the line and being unattainable and ultimately demoralizing your team? Do these specific goals drive the right behaviors along with the right results?

9. One of the most effective methods to keep your goals *"front of mind"* and relevant to your organization is to create a **dashboard** that illustrates the progress towards

---

[4] http://rapidbi.com/history-of-smart-objectives/
[5] http://goalsetting-info.blogspot.com/2012/04/smart-goals.html

your goals. These instruments should be updated and published regularly. Depending on your specific business, there are some metrics may warrant updating on an hourly basis – others *(i.e. financial results)* might be more appropriate for updating on a monthly basis. Sharing your business' performance and accomplishments with each of your associates should ideally motivate and inspire your team to remain focused and deliver results.

10. If you do not already have an **Advisory Board** in place, I suggest that you reach out to experienced independent professionals that can provide you with advice and an objective sounding board regarding your strategic goals and plans. This can be in the form of a formal, structured board that meets on a regular basis or an informal network of professionals that you can trust. Many experienced business professionals have a wealth of *lessons learned* and ***best practices*** that they have earned the hard way in their respective businesses. These boards and professional colleagues can save you and your business a tremendous amount of time and money. Of course, your Board's professional network and access to their key service providers can also provide you with a strategic competitive advantage.

As your business grows, it is valuable to periodically pause and take time to briefly reflect on what you might do differently today based on the insights and experiences that you have gained since your business was launched. Would you still launch the same products and services today? Would you hire the same associates and same skill sets? Have you gotten complacent in some areas of your business that you need to tighten up?

Transformative Innovations

While discussing the merits of building a strategy-based business, I would be remiss if I did not highlight how innovation and technology are totally transforming industries and businesses on a daily basis across the globe. There are dramatic transformational changes underway in the education, electronic commerce, energy, entertainment, financial, healthcare, manufacturing, media, mobile communications, retail, and social media sectors to name a handful. The Internet has few borders and has globalized virtually every industry. Technology has collapsed the cycle time to transform a concept into a prototype into a commercial product from years to months to weeks to days to hours. Businesses today need to recognize the vast paradigm differences and buying behaviors between baby boomers and digital natives. Included below is a small snapshot of the innovations that are driving changes in 2012 throughout B2B and B2C businesses:

3D printing	Mobile payments
Big Data	Mobile video
Bring Your Own Device	Open source software
Cloud computing	Social Media
Collaboration tools	Spatial gesture
Crowdfunding	recognition
Data Analytics	Tablets computers
Flexible screens	Touch computing
Location-aware	Ubiquitous wireless
applications	Vehicle telematics
Mobile applications	Voice recognition

I have also included an abbreviated list of innovative companies that have transformed their industries. Each of these companies started as a small business. Some of these

businesses were launched over a century ago, several within
the last decade.

Amazon	Google	Salesforce
Apple	Hulu	SolarCity
Athenahealth	Intel	Southwest Airlines
Canon	Intuitive Surgical	SpaceX
Celera Genomics	Kickstarter	Square
Costco	LinkedIn	Starbucks
DreamWorks	Microsoft	Telsa Motors
eBay	Nike	Trader Joe's
Facebook	Pandora	Twitter
First Solar	Pixar	VMware
Five Guys	Procter & Gamble	Wal-Mart
GE	Red Hat	Walt Disney

Have you envisioned your business emulating any of these
market leaders and transforming the industry where you
compete? Here are several additional innovation-related
questions for your reflection and consideration:

- Does your business strategy incorporate and embrace
  the innovations occurring in your particular industry?

- Have you identified a game-changing innovation that
  could potentially distance you from your competitors?

- Are you aware of any emerging technologies that
  could potentially make your business irrelevant in the
  next few years?

- Are changes underway that could potential disrupt the
  supply chain that you current depend upon?

- Do your associates embrace or resist changes that are currently impacting or transforming your industry?

Ideally, every entrepreneur would like to create a *"Blue Ocean Strategy" (Kim & Mauborgne)*[6], or unique, uncontested market space. Realistically this is a very challenging proposition and most businesses must thrive or survive in a market that provides prospective clients or consumers with many choices. As a business leader, you need to clearly understand and communicate your "uniqueness", focus on designing and delivering world-class products and services, and capitalize on the market opportunities that you set your sights on.

Keep in mind that innovation is a double-edge sword. While you are hard at work identifying, designing, developing, and deploying your next new innovation to differentiate your business, your competitors are most likely doing the same with varying success. Your bigger challenge is that it may not be the obvious set of competing businesses that you need to be concerned with. Most likely, it will be the next generation of entrepreneurs and business upstarts that are working feverishly to disrupt and potentially reinvent the marketplace you serve.

Summary: Your **S**trategic initiatives provide you with a roadmap and a set of goals to define your growth objectives.

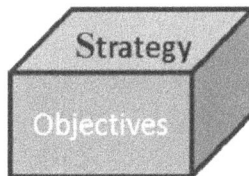

---

[6] http://www.blueoceanstrategy.com/

Creating a **M**arket-based Culture

*"Storytelling, when done right, takes a product that should have sold
$100 million worth of stuff and sells $1 billion worth of stuff."*
– Gary Vaynerchuk
*"An executive should be a realist; and no one is less realistic than the
cynic"* – Peter F. Drucker

More often than not we learn that the initial perceptions and insights we have regarding the specific market opportunity when we launch a business are not necessarily in accord with actual client requirements and our plans need to be recalibrated. You must continuously ensure that you are tuning your product strategy based on current market insights and specific customer requirements. Your business' antennae must be fully extended and at full strength with multiple sensors extracting market data from relevant and accurate information sources.

Anticipating your target clients' requirements and continuing to differentiate your products and services is a challenging job that never ends. SMB leaders should be totally immersed in understanding why your client needs your products and services, and why your client selects your products and services. Ideally, your role is to anticipate the changes in your marketplace and being proactive to respond with a goal of being first to market when possible.

One of the most impactful things that you can do as a SMB leader is to engage every member of your team as an extension of your core marketing resources. While you are not going to ask each associate to design your next advertising campaign or promotional brochure, you can promote this concept by encouraging each of your associates to continuously scrutinize your products and services offerings from your client's vantage point. Each client interaction is an opportunity for your business to capture valuable feedback. Of course this feedback needs to be filtered through your product management process, but keep in mind that the informal feedback you receive can be more meaningful than the information you receive from your formal channels.

Symptoms of Potential Market-based Challenges

I have included several questions that may expose symptoms of potential market-related challenges within your business:

- Are your associates currently engaged in an active role or passive role in marketing your products and services?

- Has your brand recognition changed or potentially eroded recently?

- Are any of your key competitors capitalizing on and reaping the rewards from new innovations to market their products and services?

- Have you been able to set aside time recently to listen to your customers, associates, and business partners – along with the social media chatter about your business and/or industry?

- Do you have a high degree of confidence that you are in a good position to anticipate and take advantage of the next new novel approach to market your products and services?

Diagnostic Questions for Potential **M**arket Challenges

It is imperative that leaders operate with a firm grasp of the specific realities in your marketplace. In reaffirming your market strategy and determining pertinent diagnosis options to potential growth market challenges, a good place to start is to spend a few minutes reflecting on your responses to the following questions:

1. How comprehensive, what level of relevant detail, and how current is your ***competitive market intelligence***? Have you invested the time and effort to ensure that you have access to relevant and valuable information to appropriate influence your marketing decisions? Do you invest sufficient time to listen to your customers and your target markets to make effective decisions regarding your marketing initiatives?

2. How effectively have you defined and communicated your ***brand***? Do you have a clear understanding of what distinguishes your products and services in your specific market *(customer value; proposition; uniqueness; innovativeness; quality; service; location; style; price; availability / distribution network; etc.)*? Have you clearly defined and articulated your ***unique selling proposition***? Have you invested sufficient time and resources to create a ***professional image*** for your business? Are you able to clearly and succinctly communicate your brand to your prospects, clients, associates, suppliers, and business partners in two to three minutes?

3. How well do you understand the various options and different approaches to **market** your products and services? Are you aware of the methods and tools your competitors are currently using? How trustworthy and reliable is your customer and contact management database? Does your customer and prospects database represent a reliable *single version of the truth* for your sales and marketing associates? Do you understand how new prospective clients discover your products and services? Is this primarily through client references, cold calls, trade shows, advertising, your website, or all of the above? What are you investing in advertising and marketing your products and services? Are you investing in the right channels? Have you embraced and invested effort in low-cost social networking tools to promote your business? Have you experimented with innovative approaches to initiate viral marketing for your brand?

4. What **feedback** mechanisms do you have in place to obtain a reality check on what is happening in your target markets? Do you have a subset of clients that are early adopters to provide you with timely and candid feedback on new products and services that you plan to introduce? Do you spend more time with clients who *"tell you want you want to hear"* versus clients who *"tell you what you need to hear"* to continue to be successful in your market?

5. Do you regularly attend **conferences**, **training**, and relevant **industry events**? Does your industry consider you an expert in your field *(i.e. via invitations to speak at key industry events)*? How often do you meet face-to-face with your clients? How effective are you at **networking** with colleagues from your industry? Do you carry professional looking business cards with you at all times for those happenstance encounters? Has your organization been

the benefactor from your *"Pay it Forward"* professional networking activities? If networking is not one of your strengths, have you engaged your staff to complement and support your industry outreach initiatives?

6. Is your organization instinctively **client-focused?** Does your staff consistently demonstrate *passion* and *empathy* for your clients? Do you practice and proactively encourage your staff to exercise *effective listening skills?* Have you implemented any staff recognition programs to publically acknowledge associates going *"above and beyond"* to support your clients?

7. Do you provide an authentic example to aspire to offer best in class levels of service and product **quality?** Have you evolved to a culture that accepts excuses? Have you witnessed *"finger-pointing"* in your operation or are your associates focused on getting to the root cause of potential problems and identifying creative and resourceful ways to prevent issues from occurring again?

8. Have you embraced a **services-orientation** across your business to deliver world-class products and services to your clients on a consistent basis? Do your associates look at job that they do in isolation, or do they have an appreciation of their role and contribution to your overarching processes of delivering products and services to your clients?

9. Have you assigned specific **product management** responsibility for your strategic products and services – or is it everyone's *(or no one's)* responsibility? Does a subset of associates within your business independently make strategic decisions regarding your products and services, or are they accountable for driving a process that makes informed, objective, and timely strategic

decisions with inputs from the right stakeholders throughout your business?

10. Since *first impressions* are extraordinarily challenging to change or overcome; do you have a realistic appreciation of the impressions that prospective clients have of your business when visiting your website, accessing your client-facing business applications, your booth at a conference, staff members at client and industry meetings, initial call from a sales associate, and/or when they call for service or support? Do you take time to disengage from your day-to-day challenges to examine your business from an outsider's *(i.e. prospective client)* perspective?

I recommend that business leaders consider the following actions to build a *M arket-based* culture.

Prescriptions for SMART Growth

1. Invest time on a daily, weekly, or at least a monthly basis towards consuming **relevant market** and **industry data** with the goal of anticipating changes in customer and market requirements and demands. Proactively participate in relevant local, regional, and national industry conferences to stay in tune with the market dynamics in your industry.

2. Ensure that you have timely **market feedback loops** along with a process to capture metrics regarding the effectiveness of each of your marketing investments. On-line survey tools *(i.e. SurveyMonkey, QuestionPro, etc.)* are an

excellent vehicle to capture both objective and subjective feedback on your products and services. Of course the most objective feedback is how clients respond to your products and services in the form of orders.

3. Design, development, implement, and institutionalize a **product management process** to address the full life-cycle of each of your strategic product and service offerings. Assign a **product** or **services manager** to each of your strategic products and services. This is not necessarily a full-time position and one staff member may be assigned the responsibility for multiple products and services. Of course, you may determine that you as the top business leader may be the most qualified candidate for this strategic role at this time for your business.

4. Develop and document *traditional marketing*, *digital marketing*, and *social media marketing* **plans**. Each target market segment typically requires a unique blend of marketing approaches to connect with your target audience and generate anticipated results. As most business owners have experienced, the types of tools that may have been effective several years ago may not be your most appropriate approach today. Your strategies and approaches for social media marketing will likely be very different than the techniques you use for your traditional marketing campaigns.

5. Design and implement a process to ensure that your **website** is updated with timely, relevant, and valuable content on a frequent basis. You also need to validate that your search engine optimization (SEO) methods are effective and achieving the desired results. There are numerous tools and techniques to help ensure that your business is relevant in the digital world. Ideally you want to keep your target audience coming back to your website

"wanting more" on a frequent basis. Regardless if your clients visit your website to order products; check on dates and schedules for events; use your publications for research; peruse your newsletter; or visit just to validate that you are a legitimate business – I can think of very few businesses that should not proactively maintain a professional website to support your business.

6. Consider authoring a **blog** on a regular basis *(at least twice per week to retain reader traffic)* to share your industry insights and help position you and your business as a leader in your industry. This is one of the most effective tools to *earn* recognition for your expertise in your specific industry. While you certainly do not need to share your "trade secrets", your blog should be focused on providing real and tangible value to your target audience. Regardless if you are a technology expert; fashion designer; restaurant owner; small manufacturer; franchise service business owner; or run a dance studio – virtually all business owners have experience and insights that are valuable to share with others.

7. Conduct regular formal and informal **briefing sessions** to educate your associates about your industry and your clients. It is far too easy to take the knowledge, insights, information, and wisdom for granted that you have captured since you conceived and launched your business. The greater the insights that your associates have, the better prepared and motivated they will be to perform as business leaders within your business.

8. **Review** your **core business processes** from the vantage point of ensuring that they are focused on servicing your clients versus other internal affairs. No business leader desires unnecessary complexity that encumbers your ability to deliver world class products and services to your

clients. It is important for business leaders to make it a priority to ensure that your operation is working efficiently and smoothly. As you add people and organization layers to your business, communication and collaboration becomes increasingly challenging. Larger businesses are more complex, but there are many examples of world-class businesses that emphasize process optimization and operate with greater efficiency than much smaller competitors.

9. Provide **education and training sessions** on *effective communications* and *effective listening* for all staff members who regularly interact with your clients. It is dangerous to assume that your associates have all the requisite training and experience to support your clients with the same knowledge and confidence as you do. In fact, associates who may exude a high degree of confidence about their ability to perform may indeed be quite naïve about your business and your client's specific needs. It is important to provide a consistent level of service to each of your clients regardless of the reason for the interaction; whom they interact with; when they contact you; and where the interaction occurs.

10. Ensure that your **sales associates** have the **qualifications, tools, information,** and **training** to meet or exceed their quotas on a consistent basis. Each sales associate is quite often in charge of creating your client's initial impression of your business. As I already stated, first impressions, especially negative ones, are extremely challenging to turn-around. Business leaders should clearly understand that successful sales professionals are extremely goal oriented. It is essential that you have established the *right goals* and provided your team with the *right tools* to position them to be successful with the *right effort* and the *right approach*. This should

result in an equation that is a win-win-win *(your clients, your associates, and your business).*

It is also important to appreciate that as your business grows, you may need to recruit different, but complementary skills sets for your sales associates. Some sales professionals are more skilled at finding prospects and introducing them to your products and services. Other sales professionals are motivated by the challenge of closing deals, while other sales professionals are passionate and skilled at maintaining client relationships along the lines of an account manager. Over time you need to build a balanced team to support the entire sales life cycle for your business.

A strong market-focus helps to ensure that your business remains relevant to your clients. It is essential to continue to evaluate whether you are offering the right products and services through the most effective channels to the ideal target markets clients for your business. The **McCarthy's 4 Ps**[7] are still relevant today for large businesses as well as SMBs:

- **Product**: Do you have a clear and realistic understanding of what your client needs or wants? Is your product or service continuing to be relevant and evolving with the needs of your clients?

- **Price**: Is your price consistent with the value that your products or services deliver to your client? How does your price compare with your relevant competitors? Are your products and services

---

[7] http://en.wikipedia.org/wiki/Marketing_mix

generating sufficient margin to cover your operating costs and position you to grow your business?

- **Place**: Are you delivering your products and services in channels that are convenient for your clients? Are there more efficient and cost effect means to offer your products and services? Are there emerging channels that you should be evaluating?

- **Promotion**: Have your advertising and promotional methods evolved with the buying habits of your clients? Do you have a firm understanding of the return on investment that you are achieving on your current promotional expenditures? Are there new marketing mediums that you have not yet exploited?

I have witnessed many businesses that have created incredible images of greatness from remarkable marketing campaigns, but totally lack any real substance from a business perspective *(i.e. "pay no attention to the man behind the curtain", Wizard of Oz)*.[8] I firmly believe in building businesses based on integrity and transparency by leading with innovative, world-class products and services supported by a compelling marketing program that effectively communicates your story to your target audience; and a demonstrated ability to execute consistently.

It is critical to stay on top of key industry trends, especially those trends that are driven by your clients and target prospects. A recent forecast from market research firm eMarketer indicated that digital advertising spending will exceed spending on traditional print advertising in 2012

---

[8] http://www.imdb.com/title/tt0032138/quotes

($37.31B versus $34.33B).[9] This trend will likely continue to accelerate during the next several years. EMarketer is also projecting that US mobile advertising will reach $2.61B in 2012, accelerating to near $11.9B by 2016.[10]

Summary: Your **S**trategic initiatives provide you with a roadmap and a set of goals to define your growth objectives; and your **M**arketing initiatives provide you with detailed plan to achieve your growth objectives.

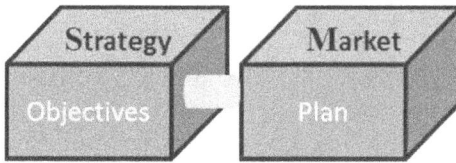

---

[9] http://www.usatoday.com/story/money/business/2012/10/18/newsweek-print-digital/1640879/
[10] http://www.emarketer.com/newsroom/index.php/emarketer-twitter-tops-facebook-mobile-advertising-revenue/

Creating an Alignment-based Culture

"The first responsibility of a leader is to define reality." – Max De Pree
"You're only as good as the people you hire." – Ray Kroc
"95% of a problem is due to the process, only 5% due to the people"
– Edwards Deming

Aligning your intellectual and financial capital based on a common set of stated goals and objectives is paramount to positioning your business for consistent growth. As a business leader you have the responsibility to maximize utilization from all available resources. Capitalizing on your opportunity to leverage your strengths positions your business to optimize your ability to service your clients.

It is amazing how much drag can be placed on your organization and ultimately your business when all of your associates are not working with a common set of goals, values, and priorities. On the other hand, extraordinary achievements occur as the alignment of all of your resources approaches 100%. Effective alignment is the result of lubricating your operation and removing any potential friction to optimize the productivity of your resources.

When analyzing the alignment of your resources, it is also important to look external to your business. Maintaining positive and proactive relationships with your key suppliers can provide you with a strategic competitive advantage. This is certainly true with your strategic partners as well. Some of your current or prospective business partners could potentially be your most valuable resources from a growth perspective. It can also be extremely powerful and profitable to be in a position to leverage your partners' client relationships that they have worked diligently to develop over months, years, or even decades.

Quite often though, I have found that business leaders grossly underestimate the effort required to developed successful partnerships. Based on my experience over the past several decades I have discovered that partnerships that actually deliver positive results are one of the hardest things to accomplish in business and rare to find great examples. You must identify common ground, goals, and synergies to achieve a *win-win-win-win-win-win* for both parties *(your business, your clients, your associates, your partner's business, partner's clients, partner's associates)*. Aligning your internal and the right external resources is a challenging effort that can deliver enormous benefits to your business.

Symptoms of Potential Alignment-based Challenges

I have included several questions that may expose symptoms of potential alignment-related challenges within your business:

- If you shared information with one of your associates and asked her to pass it along to other associates one at a time *(i.e. "Chinese whispers"[11], or the "Whispering Game")*, what message to you think would eventually get back to you?

- Have you recently had an opportunity to pause and observe your associates in action without your direct oversight? Are you pleased with the efforts and results that you see?

---

[11] http://en.wikipedia.org/wiki/Chinese_whispers

- Do you have to make an effort to initiate collaboration across various teams in your organization or does it occur naturally throughout your business?

- How quickly are your newest associates able to productively make a contribution and positive impact for your business?

- Have you encountered recent situations where someone or several associates have "dropped the ball" which ultimately resulted in "finger pointing"?

Diagnostic Questions for Potential Alignment Challenges

As a leader of your business, it is extremely important that you have a clear grasp and understanding of *"reality"* external to your business as well as internal within your business. The following questions should help provide you with an honest assessment and pertinent diagnoses of the how well the resources throughout your business are aligned.

1. As a business leader, are you proactively creating **feedback loops** to alert you of potential issues and opportunities to address in your business? Are you able to routinely allocate time to speak directly to key clients, partners, suppliers, and associates on a regular basis? Do your clients perceive that you are easy or cumbersome to conduct business? Are you able to set aside time to walk-around your operation for periodic reality checks? Do you have an appreciation of your potential blind spots

and the conscious and unconscious filters that you automatically apply to incoming messages?

2. Have you set a consistent example as a leader to create a culture with a foundation based on *integrity* and *accountability*? Are your associates accountable to follow through on assigned projects and tasks to deliver results on time, within budget, and always with integrity? To what level does each of your associates feel empowered to perform their job effectively and efficiently? Do you run your business with *transparency* or secrecy *(i.e. do your associates truly understand your successes and challenges)*?

3. Have you inspired an atmosphere and culture that embraces a *bias towards action* throughout your business? Do you feel a *sense of urgency* in how all of your associates go about their daily routine? Are the results you are experiencing consistent with your perception of the actions from your associates?

4. Does your current organization design facilitate or inhibit effective communications and *collaboration* up, down, and across your business? Do you take time periodically to assess the *chemistry* of the interactions of your team members, especially those that collaborate on a regular basis? Have you uncovered artificial barriers that are hampering effective communications across your business?

5. Have you established and communicated *clear and concise goals* for your business that each of your associates can internalize and correlate to their specific assigned roles? Can the majority of your associates express your goals in an ad-hoc one-one-one session with you? Do your associates actually subscribe and are

contributing to achieving your business goals, or are they just falling in line and doing what they are told to do?

6. Are you **communicating** effectively, consistently, and continuously across your organization? Do you continue to attempt new communication styles and approaches to ensure that you are communicating effectively and that your message is being heard? Do you lead regularly scheduled formal staff meetings as well as impromptu stand-up meetings to ensure that essential information is being shared on a timely basis?

7. Do you conduct routine **information sessions** to ensure that all members of your team continue to be informed of your mission, goals, and objectives? How well does each of your associates understand your client's perspective on your target industries? Do you routinely provide an informal forum where your associates are encouraged to openly ask you questions and share their opinions?

8. As a business leader, are you providing a confident and consistent example as a **change leader** and change agent for your business? Have you instituted effecting change management practices to realign your organization to proactively adapt to changes around you, both internally and externally? Has your organization's resiliency been tested to-date? If so, were there valuable lessons learned that you capitalized on to strengthen your business?

9. Have you instituted effective **on-boarding**, **mentoring**, *and* **training programs** to efficiently support and engage your new hires? How quickly are you able to determine if you have hired the right person for the right job at the right time? Do you monitor and measure the effectiveness of your staff training process? Are there

associates on your team that embrace and enjoy staff mentoring opportunities?

10. Have you instituted an effective **_performance evaluation_** _and_ **_feedback process_** to refocus and align all staff members across your organization? Would any of your associates be surprised with your performance feedback – i.e. are you consistently providing feedback on a timely basis? Do your associates dread or eagerly anticipate your performance evaluation sessions?

Prescriptions for **SMART** Growth

I recommend that business leaders consider the following actions to build an **_A_** **_lignment-based_** culture.

1. You should schedule time to meet with and **interact with key customers** on a weekly basis *(or as frequently as practicable)* to help you stay grounded on a continual basis. It is absolutely essential to remain firmly grounded in what you do and who you serve by not getting too distracted with internal matters and affairs. Running a business is challenging and complex and business leaders must remain vigilant to avoid distractions and remain focused on the essential elements of your business.

2. Invest the time to establish clearly articulated, concise, written **organizational goals** on an annual basis. This should not be a laborious process focused on producing a large document that no one will read. The outcome should be clearly concise and articulated goals to energize and align your organization. Your associates will rarely

exceed goals and expectations that are not clearly defined and effectively communicated. If you establish goals and expectations that do not challenge you your associates, you will most likely receive mediocre results. Setting superficial, or even worse – no goals at all – most often leads to a self-fulfilling prophecy. Business leaders should set goals that inspire your associates to deliver results beyond their own expectations. Of course there is a very fine line between inspiring your associates and demoralizing your team with unreasonable goals beyond anyone's reach.

3. Create an environment that places more emphasis on the **vital roles** for your business as opposed to specific *organizational titles*. SMBs most often require that each associate *"wear many hats"* or perform multiple job functions. Too often, employees get enamored with a specific job title or position level in the company organization chart and lose focus on what they need to be doing to delight customers and achieve your organizational goals.

    Personally, I never want to hear *"that is not in my job description"* from any associate that I am working with, especially in a small to mid-size business. SMBs have limited resources and need to count on a team that is nimble, agile, and resilient; where associates embrace opportunities to fill a void versus making excuses when asked to do something new and different. One of the methods that I have used, when it was necessary to draw an organization chart, is to draw the chart from the bottom up. I place the top executive at the bottom who has a role to support the next level of management *(next organization layer, if it exists)*, who have the role of supporting the associates performing the work every day. While most large corporate organization charts have many layers, most SMBs have the advantage of having very flat and efficient organization structures.

4. You should periodically **review** all **organizational roles** and **responsibilities** to ensure that you have *"the right people in the right seats on the bus"* for your business *(wisdom from Jim Collins' "Good to Great")*.[12] You should be seeking the optimal alignment of all of your critical resources on a recurring basis to ensure that you are able to achieve maximum performance across your business. Organizations, like your vehicles, should have periodic *"tune-ups"* scheduled and performed to ensure optimal performance for the long-term. In the case of your business, you want to ensure that you are optimizing the productivity and resiliency across your business.

    Many business owners discover that you need a different set of skills and experiences to scale a business from $1M to $5M in revenues; or $5M to $25M; $25M to $100M; $100M to $500M; etc. There is certainly nothing magic about these specific milestones – but it is well understood that business leaders require different skill sets to address the challenges and complexities as their business continues to expand and mature over time.

5. It is important that you provide a consistent and visible set of expectations regarding **accountability** for your associates. You do not need to punish your associates in a public forum, but it should always be absolutely clear that you expect full accountability for actions across your organization on a consistent basis. Ignoring feedback regarding an associate's poor or inadequate performance, especially regarding those associates that you may appear

---

[12] http://www.jimcollins.com/books.html

to favor, is a very dangerous action by business leaders and most often leads to a substantial impact the productivity across your business.

Many decades ago I came to appreciate that the *"process", not "people"* was the source of the majority of issues that occur in an organization. It is vital as a leader that you do not punish your associates for incidents that occur because a process was not well defined or institutionalized, or the associate had not been properly trained to perform his job. It is also imperative that leaders understand that showing bias or favoritism publically will have a detrimental impact on your organization's productivity. Simultaneously, it is extremely important that you proactively share **recognition** on a timely, consistent, and fair basis as earned.

6. Implement *just-in-time training* as a key element of a formal **on-boarding** or **assimilation process** for all staff members. Your objective should be to prepare all new team members to become productively engaged quickly and efficiently and fully aligned with your business' goals, objectives, and priorities. It is vital to recognize and reward your experienced associates who demonstrate willingness and the ability to effectively mentor and support their new colleagues. Clearly the sooner new associates are aligned with your business and their responsibilities; the sooner they are positioned to impact your top and/or bottom line. Coaching and mentoring your junior associates is a considerable time investment, but your efforts should deliver a tremendous return on investment in the long-term for your business.

While few leaders enjoy those discussions where you have to terminate an associate; I firmly believe in the best practice of *"slow to hire, quick to fire"*. Every hiring decision is a key decision. If new associates are not qualified and/or personally committed to perform his assigned role effectively; it can possibly wield considerable influence on your entire staff – especially if those around him have to continue to pick up the slack, or pick up the pieces behind him. SMB leaders have a fundamental responsibility to ensure that new associates assimilate into your organization on a timely and successful basis.

7. Make a commitment to conduct formal **performance reviews** on at least an annual basis. The goal should not be on producing multiple pages of written materials to stuff in a file cabinet. The focus should be on thoughtful and meaningful preparation for a candid and very personalized review of the objective contributions, challenges, and opportunities for each associate. Your preparation should be along the lines of 25% of your effort on the past performance period *(the easy component);* 50% of your effort on a plan for the next performance period *(the critical component)*; and the remaining 25% on specific actions to address any performance shortcomings and training opportunities to position the associate to assume additional responsibilities and roles *(the strategic component)* at the appropriate time.

As your organization grows, a very useful tool to enhance your performance review process is to institute *360° performance feedback*. This is a more formal process for capturing feedback on each of your associates' internal customers and suppliers, and managers and subordinates if applicable. Business leaders must take care to implement this process with clear expectations that this is an organizational performance tool to provide feedback on their colleagues to enhance their performance, not a vehicle to just to complain about the colleagues you do not favor.

If you are providing honest and timely feedback to your associates, the reactions from these performance reviews should not be a surprise to either party. Your timely feedback should include publically recognizing and *"celebrating"* outstanding individual performance along with key team accomplishments. It is also very important that business leaders demonstrate the courage to *"call a spade a spade"* when delivering performance feedback to your associates where you also have a very close personal relationship. Ignoring the obvious can be a substantial de-motivating factor for the rest of your team. Keep in mind that as tough as the conversation may be short-term, long-term you are sharing invaluable feedback to a trusted associated and demonstrating integrity to the rest of your organization.

Another essential element in this process is to periodically benchmark and verify that you are compensating your associates *(salaries)* at a fair and competitive level. You also need to validate that your periodic *salary increases* are competitive with similar businesses in your industry in your region. Keep in mind that each associate is often motivated in different ways. Your *Baby Boomers* may be motivated on elements to better position themselves for retirement; your *Gen-Xers* may be motivated by the benefits you offer to support their family; and your *Millennials* may be motivated by the amount of flex-time and vacation time you provide to your associates.

8. It is vital for all business leaders to regularly schedule informal "**dialog sessions**" with your associates to

discuss the current state of your business, challenges, competitive threats, current plans, and your results to date versus your goals. I find that the most valuable aspect of these sessions is an informal question and answer session with you as the business leader. Of course, attendance should be optional and quite often it is not practical to hold "all hands" meetings during your normal operating hours – but there are countless methods in which you can connect with your associates in an open and non-threatening dialog.

These types of intercompany interactions provide you with tremendous opportunity to demonstrate your *integrity* and *transparency* as a business leader. It is also considerably easier to inspire your team during an informal, face-to-face gathering than it is through an email message and company memorandum. As I mentioned in my introduction, time is likely your most valuable resource – but time with your associates in the right setting can be an invaluable asset for your business.

9. Considered conducting **personality surveys** and assessments (Myers-Briggs[13], DiSC[14]; Big Five[15]; etc.) for all team members to create a greater self-awareness and appreciation of the *diversity* of each of the associates within your business. There are numerous qualified human resources personnel and psychologists available in most business communities if you are not familiar with utilizing these tools or do not have access to them. My professional experience has validated that there is a direct relationship between the degree of diversity on your team and your team's creativity, resourcefulness, and resilience.

---

[13] http://www.myersbriggs.org/my-mbti-personality-type/mbti-basics/
[14] http://en.wikipedia.org/wiki/DISC_assessment
[15] http://en.wikipedia.org/wiki/Big_Five_personality_traits

I have personally witnessed the benefits of these exercises with teams on several occasions. It is extremely rewarding to hear exchanges between teammates along the lines of *"Now I understand why you responded THAT WAY when I pitched my last proposal"*; *"It is obvious to me now why the two of us look at a problem from two very different vantage points"*; *"Based on our scores, it is readily apparent why we get along so well"*; *"This exercise really shed some light on why you behave quite differently in our team meetings than the rest of us"*; to name a few.

10. I encourage all leaders to conduct thorough **investigations** *(refer to **root cause analysis** attribute section)* of consequential business **issues** and shortfalls versus quickly jumping to what appear as obvious conclusions. It is even more important to ensure that there is proper follow-up to institutionalize the insights gained from the root cause analysis so that your processes and people are re-aligned appropriately.

Another common challenge is when business leaders inadvertently ***"shoot the messenger"*** when *"bad"* or *"unexpected"* news is shared. Most of us have a knee-jerk response to surprises – but it very important, especially as a business leader, to maintain your focus, listen carefully, and not jump to conclusions and begin offering solutions before you get the facts. The last thing that you need as a business leader is to have your associates become fearful of approaching you with challenges, issues, and obstacles.

When executed well and fairly, each of these recommendations will provide you with tremendous leverage to encourage employee **retention** and **loyalty**, especially in strong economic times when competition for dedicated and high quality associates can be a significant challenge.

Of course, you have likely already identified additional *"alignment"* priorities that are important to you and your business. Many SMBs have a common thread ingrained in the fabric of their culture that is beyond the traditional scope of their business. This is quite often very personal and unique to the culture and chemistry of your business. Your associates may embrace being accountable for maintaining focus on a **"triple bottom line"**[16] *(people, planet, profit)*; proactively leading a **"green"** *(environmentally responsible and sustainable)* business with a zero *"carbon footprint"*; a business that is motivated to generate *local economic development*, or a **"socially responsible"** business actively involved in supporting specific charitable organizations; to name just a couple of examples. These very important characteristics and aspects of your culture accentuate the uniqueness of your business and are an essential factor in aligning the resources across your business.

Summary: Your **S**trategic initiatives provide you with a roadmap and a set of goals to define your growth objectives; your **M**arketing initiatives provide you with detailed plan to achieve your growth objectives; and your **A**lignment initiatives ensure that you have the right resources capable and prepared to execute your growth objectives.

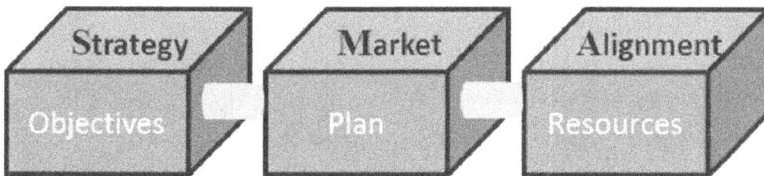

---

[16] http://en.wikipedia.org/wiki/Triple_bottom_line

Creating a **R**OI-based Culture

*"Effective leadership is putting first things first. Effective
management is discipline, carrying it out." –* Stephen Covey
"Leadership is a foul-weather job." – Peter F. Drucker

Another critical element for business growth is achieved
through optimizing the return on your precious and limited
critical resources – including your personnel, financial,
capital, and technology assets. Businesses that operate with
agility are focused on ***continuous process improvement*** to
improve performance across the entire organization.
Business leaders who aspire to increase their market presence
must inspire all of her associates and create a culture based
on optimizing the return on investment (ROI) of all available
resources throughout the business and each of your
marketing, product development, operations, customer
service, and administrative systems and support investments.

To maximize the results from your critical resources,
especially when you are planning to grow your business, you
need to ensure that you have the requisite skills to operate
your business effectively and efficiently. When a business is
initially launched in an entrepreneurial state, quite often the
founder can get by with few resources wearing multiple hats,
fulfilling multiple roles on a daily basis. As your business
grows, you need to build a team with a diverse set of skills
and experiences across your organization. You need people
that can plan; people that can create and design; people that
can develop; people that can communicate effectively; people
that can sell; people that can do; people that can account for
things; and eventually people that can effectively lead and
manage others.

Your strategic planning process should incorporate an exercise to review and evaluate your business' skill requirements against your current team of associates. Quite often you will discover that it is time to begin supplementing current resources and/or incorporating new skill sets to maximize your operating potential and growth opportunities during the next planning period.

Symptoms of Potential **R**OI-based Challenges

I have included several questions that may expose symptoms of potential return on investment-related challenges within your business:

- Do your associates quickly and naturally come together to tackle unexpected challenges and issues?

- Are the competence, productivity, and effectiveness of your associates relatively consistent throughout your business?

- How much time do you routinely have to invest in addressing issues with your suppliers?

- Have you been successful in attracting and retaining high caliber associates?

- Do your associates typically perform their assigned duties in a consistent fashion, or do you learn about team members regularly "reinventing the wheel" after the fact?

Diagnostic Questions for Potential **R**OI Challenges

Successful leaders do not shy away from embracing and confronting reality. The following questions should help provide you with an honest assessment and pertinent diagnoses of your business' emphasis towards return on investment.

1. Could you argue that you have an *agile organization* that can quickly and efficiently respond to new opportunities and challenges? Does your team routinely focus on speed and efficiency? Are your associates able to rally quickly and without considerable drama to your day-to-day challenges?

2. How effectively is your team able to *focus* on the key initiatives and tasks that have the greatest impact on your organization *(as opposed to continually put out brush fires across your organization)*? Does your latest challenge become the most recent *priority* for your team regardless of the severity or potential impact on your business? Do commitments and plans from several days earlier get lost in the day-to-day shuffle? Does your team thrive on fighting fires or getting closure on key projects?

3. Have you fostered and institutionalized a culture that is *results-oriented*? Do your associates share a sense of responsibility to complete assigned tasks and projects? Do your team members tend to focus their energy on the tasks that they enjoy the most versus what really needs to be completed to support your clients? Are you able to

pause and celebrate meeting key milestones or closing significant deals?

4. Do you believe that *operational excellence* is essential for achieving your business' mission, goals, and objectives? Would each of your associates agree as well? Have you invested sufficient time and energy to inspire a culture that embraces *continuous improvement*? Can you argue that your business is operating smarter than it was one year ago? How about three months ago?

5. What is your associates' track record in *executing your project plans* – on time, on budget, and with consistent quality – or has missing deadlines become status quo in your business? Are dates and milestones a target that get renegotiated on a weekly basis, or do your associates feel accountable for the dates and deliverables they have agreed to meet? Does your business require that you have seasoned staff members with project management skills as a *core competency?* If so, you should be recruiting for associates with a PMP *(Project Management Professional)* certification and/or equivalent experience.

6. Does each of your associates behave like *"business owners"* maintaining a keen focus on your customers while being conscientious of effectively managing and conserving cash? Have you encouraged an environment for your associates to make each decision as if it was their professional reputations were on the line? Do they make financial decisions as if they were dispensing the cash in their pockets? Do you observe your associates speaking about your business with pride?

7. Are you currently *empowering* the right team members and providing them with the right tools? My definition of the right tools includes knowledge, experience, and

information in conjunction with using the right technology as a powerful lever. Has effective empowerment positioned you to focus your time on those vital few tasks that have the most significant impact on your business? Do you feel that you can trust key staff members to be responsible for critical elements of your business? If not, what is your plan to get to this state?

8. How effectively have you been at leveraging your *suppliers* and *business partners* to support your clients? Do you view your strategic suppliers as an extension to your business – or are they each just another commodity vendor? Have you fully recognized the value that each of your strategic business partners can deliver to your clients and your bottom line? Is your business dependent on one or several suppliers providing you with unique products or services? Do you have a contingency plan in place in the event of any of your key suppliers were no longer in business?

9. How successful have you been to-date in attracting and *recruiting* the most talented and qualified staff and how energized are they to help support your business's vision, mission, objectives, and goals? Are you interviewing primarily "A" candidates, or do you have to settle for "C+" candidates that your competitors have neglected? Have you been promoting your business in a fashion that would capture the attention of prospective "A" candidates? Do you know how prospective candidates would find your business today? Have you solicited any feedback from individuals outside your business regarding how your business is perceived as an employment opportunity?

10. Do you currently capture and report on key *metrics* that monitor your team's progress against goals and client

deliverables? Do you periodically **benchmark** your business' performance against other businesses in your industry? Do you have a realistic sense of how well your business is performing and your ability to secure additional or new market opportunities? Do you maintain any market share data or routinely compare your business against your leading competitors?

Prescriptions for **SMART** Growth

I recommend that business leaders consider the following actions to build a **R** *OI-based* culture.

1. Provide the leadership to **institutionalize** your **key** internal business **processes**. This includes ensuring proper follow-through and accountability throughout your organization. The roles and responsibilities to support essential processes should be clearly defined. As a leader you should stress perseverance to get each assignment done right, the right way. Process institutionalization begins with the simple mantra, *"say what you do, and do what you say"* (*i.e. document what you do (core processes), then follow your (process) instructions repeatedly, delivering consistent results*).

   In my experience, the only sure method to create and deliver a product or service with high quality on a consistent basis is to invest the time to document how you do things and insist that your associates follow your procedures as defined. This approach does not dictate that nothing changes. In fact, ***continuous process*** *improvement* should be promoted as long as subsequent changes are institutionalized through proper documentation, training, and communications.

2. Be careful not to let position titles and organization levels interfere with efficiently delivering products and services to your clients. Instead of a focus on a formal organization chart and individual titles in a small or mid-size business, the **focus** should be **on** the "**roles** and **processes**" necessary to deliver products and services to your clients. Of course the key roles, responsibilities, and accountabilities to deliver products and services to your customers should be clearly defined.

3. SMB leaders have several options to evaluate when you need to increase your resources to address your growth. The obvious choice is recruiting and adding more **employees** to your payroll. In many situations, it may be more cost effective to **contract** specific skills – especially when the skills are not strategic to your business or it is not certain that you require these skills on a long-term basis. There are numerous sources available like *Elance*[17] to locate highly qualified part-time expertise when you need it.

   You should also periodically evaluate **outsourcing** those tasks that are not high value for your business, especially those that have little impact on the products and services that you deliver to your clients – particularly if they impede your ability to support your clients. Examples may include aspects of your financial, accounting, payroll, personnel, maintenance and facilities, and information technology support for your business.

---

[17] https://www.elance.com/

Today, you will also find seasoned professionals that are interested and will to work part-time as a **fractional executive**. This could potentially be your Chief Financial Officer, Chief Legal Officer, Chief Marketing Officer – or any key executive role that does not currently require a full-time commitment with an accompanying full-time salary. Depending on the size of your business, it may be prudent to retain a part-time executive that invests the time to really understand your challenges and opportunities versus outsourcing the function as a service. The exercise should also include a periodic review of all the roles throughout your businesses and right-sizing, realigning your organization based on your findings and conclusions.

4. Institute best practices for **effective meetings** including:

   a. Always requiring a meeting agenda, and using time-boxed agendas when appropriate.
   b. Publish agenda in advance when additional research and preparation is required to achieve meeting goals.
   c. Demonstrate leadership by your actions to establish expectations that respect all associates' time by consistently starting and finishing meetings on-time, as communicated in the meeting agenda.
   d. Only invite the appropriate associates as required by the meeting agenda.
   e. Assign responsibility to capture, prioritize, and assign responsibilities and dates to all action items discussed in meeting.
   f. Provide the leadership to take discussions off-line that do not require the time and participation from the majority of the meeting participants (*i.e. include "parking lot" for discussion topics in your minutes*).

g. Following up on action items from previous meetings to ensure that they have been completed satisfactory *(or reprioritized appropriately)*.

h. Apply the appropriate technologies for efficiency *(i.e. host environmentally friendly "green" meetings)*; while discouraging use of mobile and other technologies as a distraction *(i.e. use of social media, email, and Internet surfing should be discouraged)*.

i. Discourage *"death by PowerPoint"* style presentations, especially when presenters are reading slides to participants. Encourage creative methods to communication information efficiently and effectively.

j. Use stand-up or walk-about meetings for informal communications and collaboration with associates for discussions typically under 15 minutes.

One additional comment about meetings, while I enjoy good food as much as the next guy, I have found that breakfast, lunch, and dinner meetings are not the most efficient environments for productive discussions – but they are certainly very useful for building chemistry and camaraderie among your team members, clients, partners, vendors, etc. I typically refrain from incorporating food in meetings that target key decisions for my business. On the other hand, footing the bill to have a snack available for your informal meetings with your associates can be a powerful incentive to increase participation.

5. **Prioritize** the strategic value that each of your key **partners** and **suppliers** deliver to your business. You should assign accountability to proactively manage the relationship for key partners and suppliers ("A" list) to staff members. You should only need to invest minimal time in low priority, ("C" list) commodity suppliers. Your

business should be focused on those partners and suppliers that can provide your business with a competitive strategic advantage – both externally *(innovative products and services)* or internally *(productivity, efficiencies, and effectiveness).* In my experience, you will rarely realize any significant value in a partnership relationship without investing time to ensure that value is delivered to both parties.

6. Consider implementing a **Dashboard** and/or a **Balanced Scorecard** to establish baselines and targets, and regularly communicate your progress against your key goals. Formal Balanced Scorecards[18] *(created by Kaplan and Norton)* incorporate key metrics from a Financial, Customer, Internal Process, and Learning & Growth Perspective. Your dashboards are also an excellent source of data to benchmark your company's performance against your competitors.

   There are numerous illustrations available to assist you in developing a template for your business. I am not an advocate for investments in complex and expensive tools to maintain a dashboard for your business, but there are numerous commercial tools available. Quite you can design and update your dashboard using a spreadsheet or word processing program. The key element is to update it consistently and most importantly to use it as a tool for action in determining when course corrections are required.

7. When responding to events that occur or issues that arise, be careful not to overreact and swing the pendulum back and forth 180° on a regular basis *(most often causing another*

---

[18] http://en.wikipedia.org/wiki/Balanced_scorecard

reaction to swing the pendulum back the other direction in a short period of time). This creates a tremendous amount of disruption and inefficiency across your business. Take the time to help ensure that you are able to consistently **exercise sound judgment** and make the necessary and appropriate changes to your business processes with an emphasis on a smooth versus radical implementation methodology.

8. Periodically review the current state of your business from the vantage point of the **80/20 Rule** (Pareto principle)[19]. Is 80% of yours or your associates' time focused on 20% of your clients? Are these the right clients? Do you rank your clients relative to the value or potential that they offer to your business? Do you have a method to track how your associates spend their time?

    It is important to note that there are situations where it is appropriate and prudent to *"fire your customers"* that are not a strategic fit for your business. This may be due to the reality that you really do not offer the appropriate products or services to satisfy their needs. It may also be in recognition that your client has resolutely decided that you can never meet their expectations *(hence continuing to drain valuable time and resources from your business with marginal return)*. These situations also occur as the result of a purchasing agent who has decided that he will squeeze vendors until it is painful. Of course, when you dismiss a client, it must be conducted in a very professional manner to ensure that one client does inflict collateral damage, potentially influencing other strategic clients and ultimately your reputation.

---

[19] http://en.wikipedia.org/wiki/Pareto_principle

9. Invest the time to **educate** each of your team members so that they can clearly understand and internalize how each **associate impacts** your **top line** *(revenues)* as well as your **bottom line** *(expenses)*. You should establish an investment threshold and an investment review process to exercise consistent judgment regarding your expectations for delivering a return on your investments in your business.

10. To the extent possible, implement a **flexible work schedule** to accommodate the varying needs of your associates with the mutual benefit of improving the overall satisfaction and productivity of your team across your business. With the increasing impact of globalization and technology over the past several decades, many businesses have also implemented a ***virtual workplace*** for service and support positions – permitting associates to contribute remotely from home offices and other locations outside your immediate office. According to the US Census Bureau, during a typical week in 2010, 13.4 million people worked at least one full workday from home. [20]

In fact, there are many businesses today that used electronic tools to operate virtually without having to invest in brick and mortar infrastructure to connect their associates. Of course these options are not feasible for all businesses, but it certainly has been very successful in a number of service-based industries and provides your business with an option to dramatically reduce your overhead costs.

---

[20] http://blogs.census.gov/2012/10/09/no-commute-americans-who-work-at-home/

Creating a ROI-based Culture

One of the key prerequisites to deliver a cumulative positive Return on Investment for your valuable human and financial resources is fostering a culture that embraces **execution**. Consistent results are a direct consequence of a business culture that embraces execution through *process discipline*. Process discipline gets the job done right, on time, and within your prescribed financial constraints. Businesses that execute as planned on a consistent basis do not get distracted, yet reprioritize projects and reallocate resources as required to adapt to the needs of clients and market opportunities.

A culture that incorporates execution as one of its key building blocks includes *attention to detail, persistence, conviction, self-confidence, accountability, courage, tenacity, bias towards action,* and *dedication to get closure* on assigned tasks. Businesses that have a strong track record of executing to plan typically have strong leaders at the helm who are fully committed in both words and actions. In an era where we sometimes celebrate *"attention deficit"*, leading a disciplined organization that prides itself in her ability to meet commitments consistently is an outstanding formula to position your business to capitalize on growth opportunities.

Summary: Your **S**trategic initiatives provide you with a roadmap and a set of goals to define your growth objectives; your **M**arketing initiatives provide you with detailed plan to achieve your growth objectives; your **A**lignment initiatives ensure that you have the right resources capable and prepared to execute your growth objectives; and your **R**OI-focused initiatives ensure that your resources are properly positioned to execute efficiently to accomplish your growth objectives.

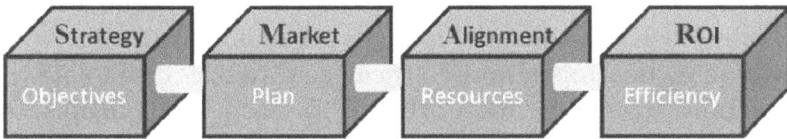

Creating a Technology-based Culture

"Never innovate to compete; innovate to change the rules of the game."
– David O. Adiefe
"In today's world, the most valuable thing that anyone has is technology. The most important thing this country can do is protect its trade secrets."
– US District Court Judge Ruben Castillo

There are very few companies that do not already rely a great deal on various technologies for the day-to-day functioning of their business. Many businesses utilize technology today for a competitive advantage in their target market. Technology is frequently used for strategic purposes as well as for tactical operational efficiencies. While technology is certainly becoming more affordable each year, thanks to fiercely competitive industries and innovative market dynamics, it is become corresponding more pervasive each year.

Another key element to growing your business is to cultivate a culture that thrives on innovation and continuously evaluates and applies creative technology and technology solutions to position your business to increase market share and potentially compete in new markets. To provide additional perspective on the emergence of various technologies over the past few decades consider that:

- Moore's Law *(Gordon Moore, Intel co-founder)* loosely stated that *"computer processors double in complexity every two years"*,[21] and his prediction has had amazing resiliency and has resulted in the engine behind the

---

[21] http://en.wikipedia.org/wiki/Moore%27s_Law

remarkable advances in computer and silicon-based innovations for the past 50 years.

- Mark Zuckerberg's *(Facebook founder)* Law of Sharing[22] predicts that the amount of information shared online with double every year.

- The number of worldwide computers in use has increased from under 5 million in 1980 to over 1.5 billion in 2010 (**315x**).[23]

- The number of worldwide cellphone subscriptions increased from 12 million in 1990 to 6 billion in 2011 (**500x**).[24]

- The number of worldwide Internet users increased from 361 million in 2000 to 2.3 billion in 2010 (**6.3x**).[25]

- The number of websites increased from under 3.2 million in 2001 to over 555 million in 20122 (**180x**).[26] [27]

- The number of worldwide email accounts is projected to increase from 2.9 billion in 2010 to 3.8 billion by 2014 (**1.3x**).[28]

- The number of US smartphone users is projected to increase from 62.2 million in 2010 to 157 million by 2014 (**2.5x**).[29]

- The number of US tablet users is projected to increase from 13 million in 2010 to 89.5 million by 2014 (**7x**).[7]

---

[22] http://www.technologyreview.com/review/426438/the-law-of-online-sharing/

[23] http://www.etforecasts.com/products/ES_cinusev2.htm

[24] http://www.infoplease.com/ipa/A0933563.html

[25] http://www.internetworldstats.com/stats.htm

[26] http://www.dlib.org/dlib/april03/lavoie/04lavoie.html

[27] http://news.netcraft.com/archives/2012/03/05/march-2012-web-server-survey.html

[28] http://www.radicati.com/wp/wp-content/uploads/2011/05/Email-Statistics-Report-2011-2015-Executive-Summary.pdf

[29] http://www.newmediatrendwatch.com/markets-by-country/17-usa/855-mobile-devices

- The number of active Facebook users increased from 100 million in 2004 to 1 billion in 2012 (**1,000x**).[30]
- The world's information is doubling every two years. In 2011 the world will create a staggering 1.8 zettabytes. By 2020 the world will generate 50 times the amount of information and 75 times the number of "information containers"... (**50x**).[31]

This is just a small sample of the rapid growth of various technologies that are likely to influence and impact your business. There are currently 72 hours of video uploaded every minute to YouTube[32]. Have you incorporated video into your marketing and support programs? Google currently processes over 100 billion search requests per month[33]. How frequently are your prospective clients searching for your products and services and how successful are you at capturing their attention? Groupon has 33 million subscribers as of early 2012[34]. Are your competitors increasing their business using Groupon, Living Social, or other local digital coupon services? Have your competitors launched a new mobile application to get more traffic to their website? If you accept credit card payments, have you invested in the latest mobile payment technology?

Today, technology has an impact on all businesses across all industries. It does not matter if you are designing innovative new robotics technology for healthcare applications, developing business analytics tools, offering facilities management software solutions, baking artisan cookies, facilitating business meetings, running a dance studio,

[30] http://finance.yahoo.com/news/number-active-users-facebook-over-230449748.html
[31] http://www.emc.com/leadership/programs/digital-universe.htm
[32] http://www.youtube.com/t/press_statistics
[33] http://searchengineland.com/google-search-press-129925
[34] http://usatoday30.usatoday.com/tech/news/story/2012-04-02/groupon-earnings/53957334/1

managing a franchise-based B2C service business, or a leading B2B consulting practice. As a SMB leader you have the choice to "create your future" or go along for the ride and hope that you able to "hang on" for the long-term. You certainly have a better opportunity to control your destiny by being aware of current trends, investing in experience in relevant technologies, and taking calculated risks to drive your business into the future.

Symptoms of Potential Technology-based Challenges

I have included several questions that may expose symptoms of potential technology-related challenges within your business:

■ When was the last time you were proud of an innovation that you implemented for your clients or internally within your business?

■ When was the last time you were able to step outside of your business long enough to participate in a business-related event with industry thought leaders primarily for inspiration?

■ Have you recently investigated other businesses or business models that could potentially seed creative ideas for your business?

■ Do your specific daily actions encourage or discourage your associates to contribute new ideas and improvement concepts?

- Do you have insights (i.e. benchmarks) into how productive your operation is versus your chief competitors?

Diagnostic Questions for Potential Technology Challenges

It is vital that business leaders institute a culture that challenges all team members to utilize the right technology, at the right place, at the right time, at the right price (ROI). In evaluating your business' utilization of technology, the following questions should help provide you with an honest assessment and pertinent diagnoses of your business' embrace of technology and innovation.

1. How open-minded are you as the business leader to new ideas and concepts that promote **new innovative approaches** to designing, developing, and delivering your products and services? Are you a technology leader or technology inhibitor for your business? What is your track record for investments in product and service innovation? What is your R&D budget for the coming year? Is technology available today that could potential turbo-charge your product and services offerings? Do you have the intestinal fortitude to follow your gut and make a strategic decision on a new direction or innovation for your business in the next 90 days?

2. Do you regularly encourage your **staff** to **contribute innovative ideas** for your products and services? Have you seeded innovation in your organization by providing your associates with new technological innovations *(i.e.*

tablets, smartphones, 3D printers, etc.) and encouraged them to suggest new creative solutions for your business? Do you have a formal methodology to capture, review, evaluate, and prioritize recommendations from your team?

3. How much time and resources are you investing in brainstorming about **technology innovations** for your business? Do have the appetite, passion, and the stamina to create insanely great products and services for your clients? Are you a *thought leader* in your field or have you delegated the advocacy role to an associate? If so, how effective has she been? Does she have the right skills and experience to make strategic technology decisions for your business? Does your strategic plan incorporate innovation as a fundamental element?

4. On the other hand, if you have totally embraced a "high-tech" environment for your business, have you potentially sacrificed essential "**high-touch**" opportunities with your clients? How successfully has the market responded to your balance of *"high-tech"* and *"high-touch"*? Have you earned the privilege of having **evangelists** for your brand outside your company? Are you continuing to *"feed"* the passion of your evangelists and remain worthy of their continued support?

5. How effective is your business at dealing with and responding to **change**? Are your associates highly resilient and typically embrace change – or do you encounter resistance each and every time you attempt to tune your business processes or incorporate refinements to the products and services that you provide to your clients? Will your associates remain on-board if you decide to drive some revolutionary changes to your client offerings or internal processes? Have your recruited any

natural change leaders that can inspire your team and earn followers through their leadership, commitment, and trust?

6. Do you have a formal process in place to efficiently *capture enhancement requests* and *new ideas* for your products and services from your clients? How do these requests get prioritized? Do your "loudest" or favorite clients always get their way – or do you have a formal, objective methodology to review, validate, and prioritize each request? Are your clients able to get feedback on their requests, or do they feel they are fruitlessly tossing them into a "Black Hole"[35]?

7. Do you have a *methodology* for identifying, evaluating, selecting, and implementing *new* innovative **tools** to support your internal business operations? Are the tools integrated? Have you inadvertently created islands of disparate technologies across your company and are you continuously building new bridges and tunnels to facilitate integration throughout your business? Are you evolving to a scenario where your business is more complicated than it should be; or a scenario where you are continuing to further optimize your operations and ability to support your clients?

8. Is your organization still primarily paper transaction-based, or have you been successful in *automating* your *core business processes* to gain efficiency and transparency across your business? Have you been able to measure the productivity improvements from your investments? Have your associates embraced your recent internal innovations or have they been successful in

---

[35] http://en.wikipedia.org/wiki/Black_hole

finding ways to circumvent your core processes using methods that they believe make their particular job easier – but that not necessarily in the best interests of your business?

9. Do you have a high degree of **data transparency** throughout your organization *(i.e. can you find stuff or has it escaped through a "black hole")?* Do you also have **data integrity** across your organization *(i.e. can you trust your data)?* Have you achieved *"a single source of the truth" (i.e. is it in one place?)* for key records for your business? Are you experiencing productivity hits because your staff members cannot locate key records?

10. How effectively are you protecting your strategic **intellectual property?** Have you put measures in place to guarantee that your business can withstand natural disasters, sudden loss of mission critical suppliers, or the unforeseen loss of critical associates? Have you properly protected your innovations from a legal perspective to provide your business with a strategic competitive advantage?

Prescriptions for **SMART** Growth

I recommend that business leaders consider the following actions to build a *Technology-based* culture.

1. Periodically perform a **market and competitive assessment** to ensure that you have a clear appreciation of the current state of the art across your industry and the types of innovations that are being introduced to your

clients and prospective customers. Most industries have extensive resources available in the form of advisory firms, conferences, journals, magazines, websites, and blogs that provide you with a vast amount of information to stay abreast of current innovations. The trick is to concentrate on the right resources from trusted contributors that deliver the greatest value to your business.

2. Schedule regular **brainstorming** and planning **sessions** with key clients and associates on your team to encourage on-going innovation planning for your product and services offerings. While many clients will not fully appreciate a new innovation until they "see it"; there is incredible value in soliciting real-time feedback on your prototypes as well as essential information to build a business case to move forward. It is extremely valuable to have access to information from experts that can *"see the future"* and position your business to anticipate and develop the next generation products and services just in time to capitalize on market demand.

3. It is essential to institutionalize a **formal product *(or services)* management process** to prioritize requests that you receive from your clients, partners, suppliers, and associates across your business. These requests should be integrated with recommendations based on your market research and competitive intelligence insights. Your product management process should be grounded with relevant research and data and driven by a consistent and objective methodology to prioritize issues, enhancement requests, and new product and service development based on a solid business-case with realistic development and implementation estimates.

4. Assign **product** or **service manager(s)** that have accountability for every key product and service that you offer to your clients. Their role is to oversee your product management process and engage your key business leaders in making informed and timely decisions resulting in specific priorities and resource allocations to continuously improve your product and services offerings. In my experience, this responsibility should have a degree of independence of the associates who actually design and/or deliver your products and services. I also firmly believe that this is also not a casual or as-required responsibility. It should be a formal element within the job description of a qualified associate or associates.

5. Create a **Technology Advisory Board** as a "sounding board" to provide objective analysis and feedback on your key external and internal technology initiatives. If you do not have the expertise and a critical objective perspective regarding your business technology and telecommunications decisions; it is advisable to engage local reputable experts and consultants. Often times, your Technology Advisory Board members can provide recommendations and assist in the evaluation and selection process for your strategic technology decisions. It is extremely challenging for technology gurus to stay abreast with everything going on in the tech space let alone a business leader with a non-tech background running a business full-time. It is extremely valuable and prudent to reach out to experts to get advice on your technology decisions and investments on a regular basis.

6. Do not become overly reliant and ultimately hypnotized by technology which can inadvertently disguise key business issues, quite often by adding unnecessary complexity. I recommend that you initially design and

implement new business processes manually at first to ensure that you have a thorough understanding of your specific business requirements. I view this approach along the lines of how software engineers develop new software applications using ***prototyping*** tools to create a representation of the final product, without all the complexities *"under the hood"*. Once the interfaces, inputs and outputs, and interconnections are validated – the engineers then go to work developing the respective technology.

This exercise can quite often be designed on a white board and implemented using manual hand-offs and communications. It is important to have a solid understanding of the potential issues and key interrelationships before you invest time, financial, and human resources to invest in and automate processes with technology.

7. Document your business **information technology *strategy*, *architecture*, *standards*,** and ***roadmap*** to ensure that you have an efficient, effective, and integrated plan for your technology investments. This certainly does not have to be an elaborate undertaking for a small to mid-size business. I will caution you though, if you ignore planning for technology infrastructure decisions, the outcome over time will likely be a complex set of loosely connected incongruent technology solutions that impede productivity and agility across your business. You should have a plan that guides you to a cohesive, integrated, and synergistic suite of technology solutions that ultimately provides you with a strategic competitive advantage.

8. Investigate "**Cloud**" computing[36] services as an option to outsource internal IT hardware, software, and the associated overhead that can be quite costly for some businesses. Be cognizant that many experts note that your computer hardware often times represents only about 15% of *"total cost of ownership"* [37] of your business technology solutions. While your hardware is often the *"tip of the iceberg"*, all the other elements, especially human resources and software licenses quite often lie as surprises below your radar screen. Cloud computing is one method if letting someone else worry about all the excruciating details required to build, maintain, and support business software solutions while you focus on your core business initiatives.

   There are hundreds of SaaS-based software solutions commercially available today that have evolved and improved over the past decade. Examples of business solutions include Sales Force Automation (SFA), Customer Relationship Management (CRM), procurement and supply chain, human resource, payroll, email, collaboration, document management, storage, and file sharing solutions. Some of these services are offered free of charge or with very low-cost, per seat options for SMBs.

9. If your business has developed **intellectual property** (IP) that provides your business with a strategic competitive advantage, you should engage a reputable patent attorney to provide you with guidance on prudent IP protection options. Filing patents can cost your business tens of thousands of dollars, but may also represent millions of

---

[36] http://computer.howstuffworks.com/cloud-computing/cloud-computing.htm
[37] http://en.wikipedia.org/wiki/Total_cost_of_ownership

dollars in new business opportunities when managed effectively. Of course you want a side dish with a heavy dose of reality close by when pursuing patent protection for your innovations.

10. Every business should have a **business continuity plan** in place today. A SMB does not require a three-inch thick, three-ring binder sitting on an office shelf, but all businesses should have formal contingency plans in the event that an unforeseen disaster or serious internal issue arises that may impact your clients and most importantly your ability to sustain your business. Business continuity plans are virtually worthless – unless they have been executed and tested. Your continuity planning should be comprehensive and cover your key associates, strategic suppliers, core business processes and supporting business systems, data, and critical technology assets. It is especially important to have contingency plans for your client-facing technologies, especially those that you likely take for granted like your phone systems, Internet connections, website, and office computers.

Contingency planning is essential for critical associates, especially the top business leader. The plans should include process documentation along with on-going methods to share institutional knowledge and train back-ups for all strategic roles in your business. "Cloud computing", highlighted above is one of the many alternatives available today that provide highly reliable computing services for SMBs, including high quality backup and recovery services at very reasonable costs.

It is appropriate at this point to revisit the power and value of **prototyping** as a method to encourage innovation, improve your speed to design new products and services, increase your time to market, provide your associates with valuable learning experiences, and solicit timely feedback from your market. Utilizing a prototyping approach enables you to quickly validate your market requirements before you invest resources in a product or service that ultimately require extensive rework or even decommissioning. This is applicable whether you are developing the next generation widget; data analytics software; or a new valuable services offering for your clients.

Over the past several years we have witnessed the evolution of low-cost software design tools and the emergence of *3D printing* technology that is now affordable for mainstream applications, including SMBs. These technologies are currently revolutionizing the concept of *rapid prototyping* and *rapid manufacturing*. 3D printers are being deployed in the automotive and aviation industries, biomedical applications, replacing hard to find – difficult to manufacture parts, along with interesting paleontology research. Software companies like *Adobe* are continuing to extend and refine their design tools to further enable the prototyping and production applications for this new printer technology.

This is an area where business leaders need to carefully set expectations as you want to clearly delineate your prototypes from your commercial products and services certainly from a quality perspective. Quite often, businesses will enjoy a subset of highly satisfied clients, potentially raving fans that will commit to investing time to evaluate a new product or service and provide you with feedback on its overall value and ability to meet their requirements. Your pioneering clients are typically happy to invest their time in exchange for pricing discounts and/or access to a new innovative concept to position them to be more competitive or increase their internal productivity. Ideally, you will have developed an iterative process to capture feedback real-time that will then be factored into the next generation prototype. Depending on the complexity of your products and services, the life cycle of your prototypes can often be measured in hours or days – versus weeks and months for a typical product development life cycle.

Summary: Your **S**trategic initiatives provide you with a roadmap and a set of goals to define your growth objectives; your **M**arketing initiatives provide you with detailed plan to achieve your growth objectives; your **A**lignment initiatives ensure that you have the right resources capable and prepared to execute your growth objectives; your **R**OI-focused initiatives ensure that your resources are properly positioned to execute efficiently to accomplish your growth objectives; and your **T**echnology initiatives ensure that you have the right tools in place to succeed in reaching your growth objectives.

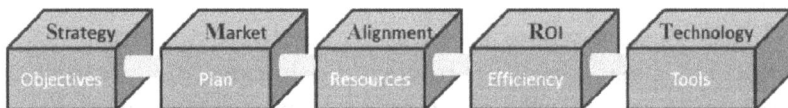

"Emphasis On" Prescriptions

"Perception is reality. Don't get confused by the facts." – Jack Trout

Most business owners would obviously prefer "easy" to "hard" and "simple" to "complex". The reality is that running a successful business is a challenging and quite often complex endeavor. SMB leaders rarely if ever have the luxury to focus on one thing. We are responsible for keeping *"all the balls in the air"*, or *"all the plates spinning"*, or whatever analogy you would like to use for carrying for leading or managing all aspects of a business. Most businesses involve keeping a lot of interrelated moving parts working efficiently while we are constantly tuning inputs, outputs, and the system that processes them.

I have identified a number of additional *"success attributes"*, or building blocks that require the attention of a business leader who strives to grow her business successfully. Following the prescription format, these attributes are much like including regular *exercise* and a healthy *nutritional diet* that includes the recommended daily dose of *vitamins* and *minerals*. These success attributes include an *(not necessarily in this sequence)*:

1. Emphasis on **accountability**
2. Emphasis on **action-orientation**
3. Emphasis on **cash flow**
4. Emphasis on **client acquisition**
5. Emphasis on **client service**

6. Emphasis on **empowerment**
7. Emphasis on **leadership**
8. Emphasis on **listening**
9. Emphasis on **metrics**
10. Emphasis on **perseverance**
11. Emphasis on **prioritization**
12. Emphasis on **quality**
13. Emphasis on **relationships**
14. Emphasis on **results**
15. Emphasis on **root cause analysis**

Obviously it is impossible to focus on all aspects of your business simultaneously – but it is important nonetheless to recognize the important elements that require your attention on an on-going basis. In this section, I will examine each of these attributes in more detail.

1. Accountability

"A body of men holding themselves accountable to nobody ought not to be trusted by anybody." — Thomas Paine

Successful businesses employ methods to instill accountability in the spirit and culture across the organization. When each associate accepts accountability for his respective actions and fully embraces his assigned role it results in an organization that operates efficiently, continuously adapts to the changes in the marketplace, and is positioned to capitalize on growth opportunities. Accountability can only be achieved when your associates fully understand the responsibilities and expectations of their role; are fully trained and capable of fulfilling that role; and have all the required information and tools at their disposal to execute their assigned duties. When this state is achieved, the results are astonishing.

Instilling accountability throughout your business, as with most things, starts at the top. The leader(s) of the organization must clearly demonstrate that she accepts accountability for her personal actions in conjunction with assuming accountability for the actions and results from the entire enterprise. As I inferred in the previous paragraph, the leaders also must ensure that each associate has the proper training, tools, and information to perform their job before you can expect associates to accept accountability for their actions. Successful leaders also *"have the back"* of their associates and avoid accusations and prosecution without fully understanding the root cause of incidents and initiatives when they do not result as anticipated.

2. Action-orientation

"Leadership is action, not position." – Donald H. McGannon

One key criterion to examine carefully when recruiting new associates for your team is *a bias for action*. A business leader that has aspirations for growth requires all team members accept the responsibility to fully understand the expectations and duties for their position and proceed accordingly. Business leaders face enormous hurdles if you regularly have your staff members queuing up in line at your desk to inquire on what to do next *(i.e. "take a number"; "Okay, next!")*. Of course a certain level of interaction and face-to-face communications is natural, required, and expected for any business; but businesses that include a team of associates with a natural inclination to take action are incredibly more efficient and productive.

Action-orientation is a critical element of the culture for any successful business. It starts by leading by example from the top and should hopefully permeate to each and every associate throughout your business. I encourage leaders to keep a close watch out for associates who can tell a great story – but more often than not demonstrate little follow-through. In other words, they are outstanding in their ability to communicate inspiring *words*, but fall short with the accompanying *actions*. It is important to note that these associates can have a very negative impact on your team's morale – especially if they are successful in convincing key leaders in the organization that they are motivated and fully on board with the goals, projects, and initiatives in the organization. In these cases, far too often their peers have to *"pick up the slack"* from their lack of commitment and follow-through. These associates can be a tremendous drag on your organization, ultimately leading to a number of negative consequences.

3. Cash flow

"Happiness is a positive cash flow." – Fred Adler

Effectively managing your businesses' cash flow is paramount for any SMB leader. Most small to mid-size businesses do not have the luxury of having tens of millions or billions of dollars of cash in the bank like several highly successful Fortune 100 companies including *Apple*, *Microsoft*, and *GE* to name just a few. Many business owners face seasonal business cycles and must be prepared to operate continuously for 365 days each year. Since 2008 many business owners have found it extremely challenging to get credit and loans to cover short-term working capital requirements and financing to support growth plans.

Positioning your business for growth requires great instincts as well as profound common sense on when to make critical short-term along with strategic long-term investments to capitalize on growth opportunities and when to be conservative with your cash outlays to endure challenging periods. Building a track record of consistently generating positive cash flow is an essential building block to building credit for your business. Strong credit provides your fuel for growth – whether it involves adding staff to support new clients; increasing inventory to support anticipated demand; or investing in new capital equipment to increase capacity.

4. Client acquisition

"The aim of marketing is to know and understand the customer so well the product or service fits him and sells itself."
— Peter F. Drucker

A blatantly obvious approach to growing your business is to focus on identifying new prospective clients for your products and services. New client acquisition is typically the primary focus for your branding, traditional marketing, digital marketing, and social media marketing initiatives. It is vital that each associate in your business should also feel responsible to identify new clients and new revenue opportunities as an essential element of their job. While maintaining a focus on your brand and the value you represent for your clients is imperative; you should continue to encourage innovative suggestions on how to extend your existing products and services as well as exploring new market opportunities that will not stretch and potentially harm your core competencies, reputation, and strategic competitive advantage.

As the top leader for your business you should pause periodically and reflect on how effective are your current marketing programs and sales process, along the lines of:

- When was the last time you stepped into "your client's shoes" and examined your solutions versus competing products and services?
- How successful are you at capturing metrics on the results of your current marketing initiatives? Are you making decisions based on your analysis of the data?
- Do your current sales quotas challenge your sales associates? Are your sales associates encouraged to be innovative in their approaches to identify prospects and close deals? Does the compensation structure for your sales associates recognize, reward, and inspire the right behaviors – are they doing the right things the right way?
- How effective are your current clients as potential referrals for prospective clients? To what extent are you able to get leverage from your existing clients?
- Is your company active in applicable industry conferences events? Are you and your associates sought out as industry experts in these events?
- Are you and your key associates investing time in pertinent professional networking events?
- Do you have an understanding of the tools and approaches that your key competitors are using to identify and land prospective clients?

5. **Client service**

"The purpose of business is to create and keep a customer."
— Peter F. Drucker
"Your most unhappy customers are your greatest source of learning"
– Bill Gates

World class client service generates tremendous new revenue opportunities with established clients as well generating compelling testimonials and new client referrals. Superior service typically results in high client retention rates along with positioning your business for tremendous after-market revenue opportunities. History has demonstrated that it is six to seven times more costly to acquire a new customer than to retain and existing one *(or the inverse, existing clients are six to seven times more valuable than new clients).*[38] This is one of the many obvious reasons to constantly reinforce with your associates that there is tremendous strategic value in delivering outstanding service for the clients that you worked diligently to earn their trust and dollars. Ideally, you want your clients to eventually become evangelists for your brand based on the value you have delivered and the trust they place in your associates that support them.

I can hardly think of a better technique to ensure that your clients are "raving fans"[39] than to provide consistent, high quality, efficient service to support the acquisition and utilization of your products and services. While innovation, features, value proposition, and price are certainly key evaluation and purchase criteria – service can many times be the primary reason that your clients remain loyal to your business. There are numerous examples to illustrate this point (i.e. Disney, Nieman Marcus, Amazon, etc.) and thousands of books available as references on this important topic.

---

[38] http://www.forbes.com/sites/gyro/2011/08/08/mining-the-gold-in-existing-customers/
[39] http://www.kenblanchard.com/Store/Books_Audios/Customer_Service/Raving_Fans/

6. **Empowerment**

"Surround yourself with the best people you can find, delegate authority, and don't interfere as long as the policy you've decided upon is being carried out." — Ronald Reagan

Empowering your associates positions your business to achieve amazing results and accomplishments, quite often beyond your wildest expectations. Empowerment ultimately requires a high degree of trust between the leaders and associates across your business. It is ultimately the product of associates fully embracing their responsibilities; possessing the competence, training, information, tools, and desire to execute the role; and feeling fully accountable for their actions *(refer to recommendations regarding accountability)*. This is certainly not an easy task and requires that leaders and all associates become proactive in their engagement and communications. Most often, it requires a considerable initial investment by the leaders – but results in an immeasurable return on investment.

Businesses are able to achieve a high level of operational excellence when each associate is empowered and accountable for their assigned tasks and responsibilities. Operating at this level positions the business leader(s) to maintain a focus on the strategic opportunities, like growth, versus being totally immersed in tactical day-to-day operational challenges. It also increases the job satisfaction, and of course contributions, from each of your associates and quite often inspires them to contribute at a high and sustained level. One telltale sign to determine if a business leader has been successful in empowering her associates is to inquire on the amount of actual vacation time she has been able to enjoy over the past two years.

7. Leadership

"Whether leaders articulate a personal philosophy or not, their behavior surely expresses a personal set of values and beliefs. ..." –
Max De Pree
"Integrity is doing the right thing even when no one is watching."
– C.S. Lewis

Obviously, leadership is an essential trait and responsibility for any successful business owner. Millions of text books, business books, publications, and articles have been published on this topic over the past century. I have highlighted several critical attributes that a leader must demonstrate to position her business to capitalize on growth opportunities the right way:

- Demonstrating *integrity* and *authenticity* in all things at all times with a consistent set of *values*
- **Inspiring** your associates by setting an example with your **words** *and* **actions** with *consistency*
- Executing business transactions in an *ethical* and *disciplined* manner every day
- Instilling trust through *transparency* in leading your business
- Leading with *passion* based on *courage* and *conviction*
- Demonstrating *loyalty* to your team with *humility* and *empathy*
- Establishing the *vision* and direction, including establishing and validating and resetting *priorities* on an on-going basis
- Exercising sound *judgment* including being *decisive* and making the tough decisions on a timely basis

- Utilizing effective **communications** and **listening** skills, recognizing when to listen, and what to say to whom, when, how, how much, and where
- Balancing **focus** on the essential *strategic* and critical *tactical* needs of your business
- Leading your business as a **realist** with a **positive**, optimistic **attitude**
- Delivering effective **change leadership** as a **champion for change** when required while building long-term **resilience** into your organization
- Nourishing a obsession for **continuous life-long learning** and **professional development**
- Checking your **ego** at the front door each day and demonstrating your ability to acknowledge and take responsibility for your mistakes
- Attaining **self-awareness** to understand your strengths and weaknesses; recognizing when you need support and insights from others; and surrounding yourself with associates who complement your abilities and possess the courage to professionally challenge your positions

8. Listening

"We have two ears and one mouth so that we can listen twice as much as we speak." Epictetus, Greek philosopher

Effective listening is quite often not an innate or finely honed skill for natural born leaders who are accustomed to giving directions (orders) instead of patiently and actively listening to others. It is crucial that you are able to listen to your associates, customers, and partners – as well as investing time to "listen" to your competitors and the dynamics in the markets that you serve.

Active listening takes an extraordinarily amount of patience and practice to master. I have always subscribed to the philosophy that you learn through listening, not talking, and that listening is an extremely valuable investment of your time. Conscientious listening:

- Goes a long way to demonstrate respect and empathy towards the speaker
- Is a skill that requires focus and a restraint on multi-tasking – a skill that many leaders feel is one of their strengths
- Requires that you hesitate to constantly interrupt others and finish their sentences for them
- Necessitates that you keep an open mind and not draw conclusions before the speaker completes a thought
- Sometimes requires that you understand how to respectfully close or redirect conversations at the appropriate time in the appropriate way
- Surprisingly may often challenge your existing paradigm about key situations or events

Another key aspect of effective listening is periodically setting aside the time to quietly reflect and listen to your own mind and hearts regarding the challenges your business faces and what you need to do to set your business on a growth trajectory.

9. Metrics

"What's measured improves." — Peter F. Drucker

You have likely surmised by now that I am a very staunch believer that developing a sound plan with specific and objective goals along with a process to measure your progress is fundamental to building and sustaining a business. I have always advocated developing a set of **dashboards** or **scorecards** to measure my progress towards achieving stated goals and objectives for the businesses I have managed. Establishing specific goals provides you with a roadmap and your dashboards provide you with an instrument to measure where you have been, what you have accomplished, and what adjustments you need to make – along the lines of the GPS devices we rely on today when we travel.

As a rule of thumb, instituting **SMART** (**S**pecific, **M**easurable, **A**ttainable, **R**elevant, and **T**ime-bound) goals[40] throughout your business is an invaluable tool to position your business to capitalize on your target growth opportunities. There are many models, illustrations, and tools available today for dashboards and scorecards that you can adapt for your specific business. Of course your dashboard is only an instrument and is only valuable if you have made a commitment to invest the time to identify the right *goals* and measure your *progress* in attaining those goals on a regular basis. It is also important to acknowledge that a prerequisite to using a dashboard to monitor your business is maintaining an **appropriate attention to details**. Accurate recordkeeping is one of the fundamental building blocks to positioning your business to capture growth opportunities.

10. Perseverance

"The only guarantee for failure is to stop trying." – John C. Maxwell
"It's supposed to be hard. If it wasn't hard, everyone would do it. The hard... is what makes it great!" – Tom Hanks, *"A League of Their Own"*

---

[40] http://en.wikipedia.org/wiki/SMART_criteria

Growth is the desired consequence of defining and communicating a vision supported with goals, detailed action plans, and a commitment and proper follow-through to execute your plans. Many leaders suffer from *"attention deficit"* and it is important to acknowledge your strengths and weaknesses and surround yourself with people who complement you and position you to focus on those tasks that play to your strengths while delegating other tasks to qualified associates.

Perseverance is a requisite skill for businesses that desire to grow their market presence and is exemplified by an organization's ability to focus on key tasks and avoid the daily distractions that can quite easily take you off course. Perseverance is the foundation of institutionalizing key changes to processes, procedures, and organization structure to support your clients and strategic initiatives. Perseverance is also the fuel that enables your business to withstand new competitive threats and unforeseen challenges and obstacles that your business will constantly face as you grow your business. Empowerment is an amazing ally to perseverance, as it encourages your associates to make timely, but grounded decisions in response to unexpected events and outcomes while continuing to focus on the desired final outcome.

11. Prioritization

"Focus on a few key objectives ... I only have three things to do. I have to choose the right people, allocate the right number of dollars, and transmit ideas from one division to another with the speed of light. So I'm really in the business of being the gatekeeper and the transmitter of ideas."
— Jack Welch
"When you try to be all things to all people, you end up being nothing."
— Al Reis

I have run into far too many agonizing situations where a business leader insists that everything is a top priority and refuses to do her job to prioritize specific projects and tasks for her associates. My interpretation in these situations where *"everything"* is the top priority is in reality it is synonymous with *"nothing"* is a priority at this time. Establishing the right priorities and more importantly deciding on what items are **not** essential for your business at this moment is one of the most impactful jobs that a leader can do for the organization. This is not a simple job in almost all cases, but most of us understand and accept that a leader's job is rarely easy.

There are numerous methods and tools that can be deployed to assist in the prioritization of projects and tasks for your business. I have always been an advocate of *"keeping it simple"* for your associates, or at least not over-complicating the prioritization process which may ultimately get in the way of getting the job done. Many businesses can manage and prioritize their initiatives within a spreadsheet or word processing document while other businesses may need to use more sophisticated tools due the volume or nature of the initiatives that they face on a daily basis. I firmly advocate that saying *"No"* is one of the most essential aspects of a leader's job. In order to keep your business on a growth trajectory, it is critical that you regularly review, reassess, and reprioritize that key projects and initiatives across your business.

12. Quality

"Be a yardstick of quality. Some people aren't used to an environment where excellence is expected." – Steve Jobs

Designing, developing, deploying, delivering, servicing, and supporting your products and services with consistency is one of the most essential elements and quite often a minimum requirement to maximize your growth potential. In many cases, quality can be more of a potential liability than a prospective asset to your business as many industries have placed an intense focus on quality-related initiatives since the 1980's.

It is critical for all business leaders, especially SMB leaders to cultivate a culture and a passion for delivering quality products and services in each of your associates. I continue to be an advocate of the *"Say what you do, Do what you say"* philosophy prescribed by the ISO 9001 quality management systems standard.[41] This is a very simplified, concise, but powerful message to share with your team to ensure that you are ultimately supporting your clients in a reliable and consistent fashion. The bottom line is while your quality initiatives may not be your top objective in your strategic plan or a recurring line item on your weekly agenda – lack of focus and attention in this area can be a strategic liability ultimately impeding your growth potential with a single serious instance.

13. Relationships

"The most important single ingredient in the formula of success is knowing how to get along with people." — Theodore Roosevelt

Personal relationships are extremely complex, unpredictable, sometimes volatile, and naturally essential for any business to succeed. Of course all business relationships are ultimately personal relationships. Business leaders must continuously focus their time and energy to build effective and productive relationships with their associates, clients, suppliers and service providers, partners, and key industry associations. I

---

[41] http://www.iso.org/iso/catalogue_detail?csnumber=46486

have developed a formula that summarizes the key elements of building successful professional relationships as follows:

Effective Relationships f Trust f Effective Communications

In other words the building blocks of developing effective relationships is effective communication between the two parties which builds trust which ultimately lays the foundation for a successful business relationship. The underlying basis of trust for a successful professional relationship is a conscious and proactive investment in effective communications. I also believe that sound business relationships are not developed and sustained through impersonal communications like electronic mail and phone calls. Trust is the result of genuine personal relationships that are manifested through a series of productive interpersonal interactions. These interactions include speech and body language which are the key influencers in communicating a message to another person. Once trust is established between two parties, then electronic communications can certainly be an effective and appropriate method to continue to build and sustain your relationship.

14. Results

"The two most important requirements for major success are: first, being in the right place at the right time, and second, doing something about it." – Ray Kroc

Another critical skill required for leaders is being aware of their potential blind spots. I suspect that you may have worked with associates that are extremely skillful in telling you *"what you want to hear"*, not necessarily *"what you need to know"*. Most often the intent is not to deceive you as much as it is a bi-product of an associate working extremely hard to please his boss. At the end of the day it is imperative that business leaders actively seek, confront, and deal with reality – not with perceptions, and quite often not with what you would like to hear. As you interact with your associates, it is essential to filter out potential smoke screens and remember that it's not about the words or the intent. The dialog should be focused on the results, and then of course *corrective actions* and *lessons learned* if the desired results are not achieved.

You will most likely hear countless reasons from your associates regarding why specific tasks or milestones are not achieved, but as a leader you must continually focus on actual results and respond accordingly. It is also important to analyze and evaluate results from different angles and engage your team members to share their perspectives on cause and effect. Bottom line is that business leaders must maintain a constant focus on results to position your business to continue to grow and prosper.

15. **Root cause analysis**

"Learn from the mistakes of others – you can never live long enough to make them all yourself." – John Luther

It is invaluable for business leaders to invest the time to understand why things went wrong; did not produce desired results; did not operate consistently; or did not produce a consistent outcome. Root cause analysis techniques are a very effective method to resolve problems on a permanent basis. One technique is to use an approach of asking *"Why?"* five times (from Sakichi Toyoda of Toyota Motors)[42] to understand and uncover the "cause and effect" relationships that resulted in problems. Another powerful process is to

---

[42] http://en.wikipedia.org/wiki/5_Whys

formally identify, analyze, evaluate, and document *"Lessons Learned"* based on key events that impact mission critical processes in your business. It is important to take action on a timely basis to eliminate known problems and ultimately institutionalize any change that you have identified as a result of your analysis.

This is where key attributes like *perseverance, accountability, quality,* and *metrics* are critical differentiators. Quite often designing and implementing a permanent fix to problems feels like a distraction to the already overwhelming tasks that both leaders and associates face each day. The ability to proactively identify, address, and implement permanent improvements to key issues quite often will distinguish those businesses positioned for growth versus other businesses that continue to "tread water" in their marketplace.

"Just Enough" Prescriptions

While formalities like organization structure, policies, and procedures are necessary to some degree for any successful business, it is imperative that there is not too much focus on certain aspects of growing a small to mid-size business that ultimately impedes growth. There is a fine line between *just enough* and *too much* of many business activities. This section includes a set of prescriptions on ***"doing things in moderation"***. Experienced leaders develop good judgment based on their intuition on just how much effort and energy should be expended on various initiatives across her business. Based on my experience, I recommend that leaders implement:

1. *Just enough* **communication**
2. *Just enough* **governance**
3. *Just enough* **information**
4. *Just enough* **infrastructure**
5. *Just enough* **oversight**
6. *Just enough* **planning**
7. *Just enough* **process**
8. *Just enough* **resources**
9. *Just enough* **structure**
10. *Just enough* **technology**

While each of these prescriptions potentially represents a value-add to your business, *"too much of a good thing"* can also be a detriment to your business. I present an additional set of guidelines to consider for each of these prescriptions in more detail.

1. **Communication**

Effective communications is essential, but too much communication done the wrong way can result in an organization that is paralyzed from *information overload*. If your associates are spending the majority of the time reading and responding to email, especially messages that are not directly associated with their specific responsibilities – then you likely have a productivity problem that needs to be addressed. Too much communication begets information overload which begets loss of focus which begets ignored priorities which begets fewer tangible deliverables which begets dissatisfied business leaders and clients.

Non-productive communication warning signs that business leaders should be on the lookout include:

- Multiple email replies between associates in the same office *(e.g. get up from your desk and discuss the item in person with your colleague)*
- Practice of cc'ing or bcc'ing associates that do not need to be involved in the discussion
- Use of formal structured correspondence when a simple informal discuss will suffice
- Using email to discuss a topic that requires personal collaboration among associates, or as an avoidance for face-to-face discussions
- Long rambling email messages that challenge the reader to understand the action required or specific message conveyed
- Developing formal PowerPoint slides to discuss a topic that can be easily conveyed in a team meeting

- Staff or team meetings without a structured agenda that continue long after useful intent
- Meetings with participants who are not prepared to engage in the discussion to support effective decision-making (i.e. meeting should be rescheduled immediately)
- Lengthy discussions that take place in team meetings to resolve issues that should involve a small percentage of the meeting participants
- Using email to air disagreements and emotional arguments that need to be discussed face-to-face

2. Governance

Instituting enough governance throughout your organization ensures that your business can continue to operate with integrity and within the various laws, ordinances, and regulations that govern your respective market. Too much governance can absolutely stifle productivity. On the other hand, no governance at all can ultimately lead to unpleasant surprises and unfortunately can result in having to shut down your business. Regrettably I am too familiar with small and mid-size businesses that had to lay off their associates and close their doors due to embezzlement that had occurred unbeknown to the owners.

Ample policies and procedures should be in place to ensure that your associates comply with any legal, regulatory, and compliance policies that apply to your business. It is the leaders' responsibility to ensure that there are clear separation of duties, especially when it comes to handling cash and key financial records that can easily be compromised or tampered with based on some minor collusion among a couple of associates. Empowerment is a desirable state – but all organizations require just enough checks and balances to ensure that records are kept with integrity and that your business is in compliance with applicable legal guidelines.

3. Information

While having relevant, factual, and timely information is essential to making sound business decisions, it is easy to fall into a trap where you become immersed in data to the point where it is almost impossible to make key business decisions on a timely basis *(sometimes referred to as analysis paralysis, drowning in data, or information overload)*. This is a case where assembling a diverse team of associates can truly be an asset. Whereas some of us are extremely analytical and rely heavily on data to support analysis to arrive at a decision; some of us are very prefer to follow our intuition and past experiences to make decisions and would prefer not to be distracted with a lot of additional peripheral information.

A recent report by IDC forecasted that 2.7 zettabytes *(27 followed by 21 zeros)* of digital information would be available on the Internet in 2012.[43] Each of your associates can spend a lifetime searching for information on the Internet to support your business. On the other hand, many entrepreneurs are accustomed to being extremely agile and making decisions "on the fly", but as your business and organization grow more complex, you also need to understand that the consequences of each decision become a more significant factor. This is another example of where you need to continuously apply good judgment regarding your understanding of the risks and rewards of a particular decision; determining how much information is enough; and

---

[43] http://www.idc.com/getdoc.jsp?containerId=prUS23177411

make the most prudent decision possible with the facts that you have.

4. Infrastructure

As your organization grows, you will need to plan and invest in additional support, facilities, and technology infrastructure to enable your business to grow. There are a number of alternatives to consider when you are dealing with the growing pains from the success you have had in scaling your business. One option when confronted with having to acquire addition floor space is permit some of your associates to work virtually from their home office, especially if their job requires them to travel frequently. Another option is to assign shared office space, or *hotelling*, for associates that are not required to be in your office on a full-time basis.

While there are certainly situations where it is important for associates to collaborate and function seamlessly as a team, there is also a strong business case for the personal productivity and freedom that associates can realize by working from a *home office*. In fact, there are many businesses that have been launched in the past decade that operate without any investments in real estate and the overhead costs associated with maintaining a facility. Of course if your business produces a product or offers a consumer-based service where your clients come to you – running a virtual business is most likely out of the question.

You should also periodically examine opportunities to potentially outsource functions that are not mission-critical to your business. For many SMBs, it is often more cost effective to contract experts in particular fields as you need their services versus adding them to your payroll on a full-time basis. Inevitably, you will reach a milestone in the growth of your business where it becomes more cost effective or a particular role becomes more strategic to staff in-house versus contract the services.

Regardless, there are often a number of viable alternatives to evaluate when you arrive at an intersection that requires that you consider adding new infrastructure to your business (overhead staff, real estate and facilities, technology, etc.). While many of these decisions are tactical, a number of these decisions will be a very crucial element of your strategic growth plan.

5. Oversight

Another fine line in managing a successful business is implementing enough structure, organization, and oversight to ensure that your business is operating effective, but not to the point where you start to impede your team. Ideally, you want to lead a frictionless operation, but it is virtually impossible for this to occur in a totally autonomous organization. You should strive to empower all of your associates applying the right amount of structure, training, information, communications, and tools to create an efficient, productive, and hopefully inspired team.

It is almost guaranteed that surprises will occur if you are too disconnected from the key processes and associates across your business. Too much oversight will not only impact your personal productivity, but also impact your associates' ability to perform their jobs. From your associate's perspective, they need to respect that you know what is going on in your business and appreciate that you are accessible and available if and when needed to address issues and opportunities.

6. Planning

I am passionate about cultivating a culture with a focus on **execution**. While I have preached throughout this book the importance of establishing goals, objectives, plans, and metrics – it is easy to over compensate in a reaction to initiatives that have gone off course and to place too much emphasis on the up-front planning to avoid another similar incident. Developing a plan or roadmap is certainly required, but it is important to also recognize that it is virtually impossible to anticipate ALL the variables, challenges, and obstacles that you will face. There is tremendous value in learning by doing, and most importantly capturing lessons learned, capitalizing on new insights, and incorporating them into your plan.

Quite often you are planning for failure if you do not have a plan and a method to align your resources so that everyone is working towards common goals and objectives. While being a huge supporter for effective project management practices and holding project managers accountable for results, I am not a huge advocate for complex project management tools. There are certainly complex, large-scale projects *(i.e. implementing an Enterprise Resource Management (ERM/ERP) solution)*[44] that need a comparable tool, often times a spreadsheet tool or conference room whiteboard might be efficient to get the job done. One key thought to keep in mind is that your competitors may beat you to the finish line if you spend all your time focused on developing the perfect plan versus getting to the finish line first.

---

[44] http://en.wikipedia.org/wiki/Enterprise_Resource_Management

7. Process

"If you can't describe what you are doing as a process, you don't know what you're doing" – W. Edwards Deming

Of the many things that I have advocated in this book, I have been a student of process analysis, design, implementation, and institutionalization for many decades. It is also quite important to identify and document your key business processes in order to position your business to scale. If you desire to create efficiencies in your operations to permit higher throughput, you need to define and document repeatable processes. When I reference documenting a process, I recommend that you institute just enough documentation to provide a set of procedures for your associates to follow. It is even more important that you have instituted a process to document subsequent changes to your process, i.e. institutionalizing your changes, so that you can ultimately capitalize on the improvements that you have worked hard to identify.

While strict adherence to your key processes should help to ensure consistent outcomes in the form of high quality processes and services; procedures that are too stringent can also encumber your organization to capitalize on opportunities to grow. When a process starts to feel like bureaucracy, then you have likely implemented too many guidelines and constraints. A key element of an optimized organization is having open communication lines with associates supporting your processes and continuing to make prudent refinements based on the internal and external feedback you receive. Of course there are some processes that may feel bureaucratic, but are required by a regulation or federal or state legal statute.

8. Resources

Determining the optimum staffing levels for your business is a significant challenge, especially for small to mid-size businesses. Ideally, you want to have just enough of the *right skills*, at the *right time*, in the *right place* to tackle each specific requirement that your business faces. Initially, having the right associates who can stretch to meet your business requirements and challenges as needed is ideal *(i.e. you need a pitcher, infielders, and outfields to field a team)*. As your business reaches a certain level, it is no longer practical to assume that your current associates can respond to each and every new challenge that you confront *(i.e. you need starting pitchers, relief pitchers, catchers, 1st basemen, 2nd basemen, …, left fielders)*. While it is costly and inefficient to have players sitting on your bench in anticipation of customer demand; it can also be perilous to delay hiring additional staff when you need them and face the risk of burning out and potentially losing your current associates.

The challenge is recognizing when the time is right to begin your transition from a team of passionate utility players to building a team of associates with unique and complementary skills. Over time, you should be developing a strategic resource plan as a roadmap to recruit the right skills just in time to meet the demands of your expanding business.

It is also important to note that you need to pause periodically and review if you have the right people in the right jobs. Are your associates challenged? Do they have the required skills and training to perform their role effectively? Are they passionate about the role? Are you developing future leaders to fill new voids as you scale your business? Is each of your associates in harmony with the culture and values that you have developed for your business?

9. **Structure**

As your business grows and becomes more complex, the founders have to begin to design, implement, and staff a more formal organization structure to more efficiently delegate and manage the essential roles, tasks, and projects. I suggest that you continue to keep the organization as lean and with minimum layers as long as possible. You can make a mistake by not responding to business needs quickly enough and permitting your organization to become dysfunctional It is also important to not go too far with this exercise and create more structure than is needed for the current workload and putting a drag on your associates.

As your business scales, you will no longer be in a position to effectively manage all your resources and you will have to create more structure and a chain of command to manage your business and more importantly continue to proactively prioritize the vast number of tasks and initiatives.

10. **Technology**

I spent a significant portion of my career implementing business technology solutions to improve my company's or clients' productivity. While I continue to be a huge proponent of implementing business technology to increase the efficiencies and capabilities across your business, I am simultaneously adamant that you should implement *just enough* technology to achieve your goals and not to be lured into implementing solutions that add unnecessary complexity and overhead costs to your business.

One of the areas where an increasing number of options exist is in the area of technology and business systems infrastructure to support your operations. As the number of highly configurable business solutions have increased dramatically over the past two decades, I am also a big advocate of taking advantage of *Cloud-based* or *Software as a Service* (SaaS) computing solutions as an alternative to acquiring, implementing, and support core IT services (email, document processing, document management, communications and collaboration tools, etc.) along with core business systems (customer management, website hosting, order processing and fulfillment, etc.). Many of these vendor-supplied and hosted service offerings offer an attractive ROI – but that will vary greatly business-to-business depending on the size of your business and the industry that you participate.

It has been my experience that implementing a comprehensive software suite *(i.e. an enterprise solution that includes your client database, order processing, client invoicing and receipts, process automation, supply chain, payroll, accounts payable, accounting, etc.)* is most often considerably less expensive than attempting to integrate multiple software packages internally. There are too many variables with different life cycles *(continuous upgrades for hardware, software, infrastructure, facilities, etc.)*. Far too often, I have also found that it is substantially more expensive to develop your own customized software solutions in-house unless you have very unique mission-critical requirements for your specific business.

As I noted earlier, I am not an advocate of using sophisticated project management software for a small project or project that is not overly complex when a spreadsheet will do the job. One method to improve staff productivity and a positive ROI is to standardize on the communications, collaboration, and productivity tools used by your associates. These tools include your email, conferencing, word processing, spreadsheet, presentation and design tools to run your business.

There are some financial and time investments that you absolutely cannot avoid as a business leader. It is essential that you have implemented sound cyber security technology *(i.e. firewalls, virus protection, data backups, spam filters, etc.)* and business practices to protect your business. It is also very important that you rigorously protect and secure key intellectual property that is strategic and vital for your business.

Bottom line, technology can produce a tremendous return on investment for your business – but you should remain focused on the ROI and be careful not to become enamored with the latest and greatest technology innovations. In other words, implement technology for business sake, not technology for technology sake.

Conclusions and Implementation Plan

"May the Force be with you." – various characters from Star Wars

We have covered an extensive and synergistic set of recommendations and action items to position business leaders to confront challenges and obstacles head-on while you scale your business to capitalize on new market and business opportunities. The major themes are summarized below:

- Define a set of specific **S***trategic* goals with supporting tactical plans to ensure that your business remains competitive and profitable for the long-term
- Develop reality-centered **M***arketing* plans to focus your resources on key opportunities in your target markets
- Ensure that all of your vital resources are properly prepared, positioned, and **A***ligned* to power your business forward
- Implement processes, checkpoints, and milestones to maximize your **R***eturn on investment* on all of your projects and corresponding financial and human resource commitments
- Validate that you are using the optimal approaches and **T***echnology* innovations as a lever to achieve your goals smarter and faster than your competitors

Obviously, there are numerous other considerations that you have to factor in as I shared in the *"Emphasis on"* and *"Just Enough"* sections. Each of those key attributes requires your attention in varying degrees at the appropriate time. The overarching factors include *prioritization, focus*, and *perseverance* to help you address the *what?, why?, when?, where?*, *how?*, and *how much?* questions that will constantly confront you.

At this point, you may be ruminating over a series of questions in your mind along the lines of... *where do I start?*; *what do I do first?*; *when do I do it?*; and *how much can I do?* If you are not certain how to get started to proactively address your current challenges, I recommend that you commit to a *six month* review and implementation plan. Initially, I suggest that you focus on your **S***trategic* goals and objectives in the first month; followed by a review of your **M***arketing* strategies, goals, and plans in month two; then put your attention towards **A***ligning* all of your vital resources in month three; next focus on evaluating and instituting the right mechanisms to ensure that you understand the **R***OI* on your investments in the fourth month; and finally conducting an assessment of how your business is capitalizing on the latest relevant innovations and new **T***echnologies* in month five.

I recommend that you use the sixth and final month to develop specific goals and plans for your six-month, twelve-month, and 18-month planning horizons with an overarching objective of having plans to execute that also include specific accountabilities for each of your associates. It is important to pace yourself so that you are allocating sufficient time in each area – but at the same time, *"time is money"* and you may be leaving too much on the table if you invest too much time in the planning versus the execution phases.

If you and your business are currently on a fast-track growth trajectory *(i.e. planning to scale your business 10x in the next 18 to 36 months)*, I suggest that you review and execute all the **SMART** Growth recommendations in the next 90 days. While this may appear to be a very challenging task is it absolutely achievable when initiated by an inspired business leader who has a clear vision and plan for her business.

Of course, any experienced business leader recognizes that maintaining a consistent focus on each of these elements is a daunting and unnerving task. The bottom line is when you are able to lead an agile organization with the right focus and balance on the specific needs of your business; you will be positioned to deliver **SMART** Growth that will benefit your clients, associates, suppliers, partners, and other key stakeholders.

The tools, insights, and action items incorporated throughout this book provide you with a **SMART** approach to efficiently and successfully scale your business to achieve **GROWTH**. Your results should include building a business that embraces:

- **G**oals-Orientation
- **R**esults-Orientation
- **O**perational Excellence
- **W**orld Class products, services, and solutions
- **T**rust from your associates, clients, suppliers, & business partners
- **H**igh Growth trajectory, sustained for the long-term

It was my objective and inspiration to provide you with insights and specific action items that would enhance your confidence, courage, and conviction to lead your business into the future and capitalize on the tremendous opportunities that lie ahead, both visible and invisible. Many entrepreneurs are born with the DNA that inspires them to make a difference in their world. I certainly hope that the

Conclusions and Implementation Plan

time you have invested to read my recommendations have further motivated and prepared you to lead your business towards a new frontier, hopefully beyond your wildest dreams *(to infinity and beyond!)*[45].

---

[45] http://www.amazon.com/To-Infinity-Beyond-Animation-Studios/dp/0811850129

Your Prescription for **SMART** GROWTH

The following section is a summary in checklist form of the action items prescribed in the chapters that described success factors for a **Strategy-based, M**arket-based, **A**lignment-based, **R**OI-based, and **T**echnology-based business.

Creating a **S**trategy-based Culture

- ☐ Update your subscriptions and sources for **key market and industry data.**

- ☐ Revalidate the foundation of your **strategic competitive advantage.**

- ☐ Define your **growth expectations** for the next planning period.

- ☐ Implement an evergreen **strategic planning process.**

- ☐ Update the **strategic plan** for your business.

- ☐ **Validate** your strategies and implement adjustments as required.

- ☐ Establish **SMART goals** for your business.

- ☐ Define and document corresponding specific and measurable **individual goals** for each associate.

- ☐ Implement a **dashboard** to measure and communicate the progress towards your goals.

- ☐ Assemble a business **Advisory Board** to support effective decision-making.

Creating a **M**arket-based Culture

☐ Review **relevant market** and **industry data** to validate your marketing programs.

☐ Introduce timely **market feedback mechanisms** to measure the effectiveness of your marketing programs.

☐ Implement a **product management process** to manage the life-cycle of each of your strategic products and services.

☐ Develop and document *traditional marketing*, *digital marketing*, and *social media marketing* plans for your business.

☐ Implement a program and responsibilities for timely and relevant **website** updates.

☐ Publish **Blog** updates on a frequent basis with the goal of being recognized as an *industry leader*.

☐ Conduct regular formal and informal **briefing sessions** with your associates to share industry and client insights.

☐ Focus your **core business processes** with a *bias* towards supporting your *clients*.

☐ **Educate** your *staff members* on *effective communications* techniques and *interactions* with your *clients*.

☐ *Invest in your* **sales associates** to position them to meet or exceed their quotas on a consistent basis.

Creating a Alignment-based Culture

☐ Invest time to meet with and **interact with key customers** on a regular basis.

☐ Establish clearly articulated, concise, written annual **organizational goals** as a roadmap for your associates.

☐ Focus on defining **vital roles** rather than *organizational titles* to support your business.

☐ Periodically **review** all **organizational roles** and **responsibilities** and realign as required.

☐ Instill **accountability** for all of your associates.

☐ Develop a formal **on-boarding process** for all new associates.

☐ Conduct formal **performance reviews** on an annual basis.

☐ Schedule regular informal **"dialog sessions"** with your associates.

☐ Conduct **personality surveys** periodically to increase the appreciation of the *diversity* across your organization.

☐ Investigate critical business **issues** thoroughly with the goal of identifying lessons learned and instituting changes to address the root cause.

Creating a ROI-based Culture

☐ Invest the time to **institutionalize** your **key** internal business **processes**.

☐ **Focus on** the **"roles** and **processes"** versus position titles to deliver products and services to your clients.

- ❑ Carefully **evaluate** the **options** to **add additional resources** to your business.

- ❑ Institute best practices for **effective meetings** across your business.

- ❑ **Prioritize** the value that each of your key **partners** and **suppliers** deliver to your business and assign resources to support these business relationships according.

- ❑ Implement a **Dashboard** to establish baselines and targets, and regularly communicate your progress against your key goals with your associates.

- ❑ **Exercise sound judgment** in response to *unexpected incidents and events*.

- ❑ Subscribe to the **80/20 Rule** to ensure that you are allocating the appropriate resources to the right things at the right time.

- ❑ Invest time to **educate** your associates about your business so that they can clearly understand and embrace how they **impact** your *top and bottom line*.

- ❑ Implement a **flexible work environment** that addresses the needs of both your clients and your associates.

Creating a **T**echnology-based Culture

- ❑ Initiate periodic **market and competitive analysis** to remain connected with your clients' requirements and relevant industry trends.

- ❑ Schedule frequent **brainstorming sessions** to encourage *innovation* across your business.

- ❑ Institutionalize a **formal product management process** to efficiently prioritize new requests to keep your products and services in concert with the current state of the industry.

☐ Assign a **product manager**(s) to oversee each of your key products and services.

☐ Implement a **Technology Advisory Board** to provide objective analysis and feedback on your key technology initiatives.

☐ Initially **design new business processes manually** in advance of automation to ensure that you have a thorough understanding of your specific business requirements.

☐ Develop a **technology strategy, architecture,** and **roadmap** for your business.

☐ Evaluate "**Cloud computing**" as an option to reduce costs and improve service levels.

☐ Carefully protect and manage your business' **intellectual property** (IP).

☐ Document a comprehensive **business continuity plan** to proactively protect your business.

I have also included a series of questions in checklist form that represent the *"Emphasis On"* and *"Just Enough"* business attributes to scrutinize across your organization periodically.

"Emphasis On" Attributes

☐ Does each of your associates embrace and demonstrate **accountability** for their assigned roles?

Your Prescription for SMART GROWTH

☐ Have you created a culture of **action-orientation** without you having to be directive?

☐ Has generating positive **cash flow** become *business as usual* or does it continue to require a considerable amount of your attention?

☐ Have your strategies, methodologies, and sources of new **client acquisition** targets continue to produce positive results to support your growth plans?

☐ Do your existing clients provide you with unsolicited feedback on the quality and overall value of your **client service** initiatives?

☐ Do your associates welcome your delegation and **empowerment** efforts or does it make them uncomfortable and insecure?

☐ Are you receiving feedback that your **leadership** style and approach is inspiring your associates in the form of producing the desired results for your bottom line?

☐ Have you been making time to exercise effective **listening** skills with your associates, customers, and business partners?

☐ Have you identified the appropriate **metrics** that enable you to effectively measure your progress to reach or exceed your growth projections?

☐ Are your associates consistently demonstrating **perseverance** to tackle the challenges and obstacles that come their way on a daily basis?

☐ Have you successful in instilling a culture that demands **prioritization** and alignment across your organization?

☐ Does each of your associates embrace **quality** as an explicit and unequivocal expectation for her assigned role?

❑ Do you have positive professional **relationships** throughout your business or are their several cliques that result in contention across teams?

❑ Are your associates inspired and drive to deliver **results** consistent with your strategies and goals?

❑ Do your associates choose to conduct a **root cause analysis** of issues and problems that arise versus finger-pointing as the easy way out?

"Just Enough" Attributes

❑ Does **communication** flow seamlessly throughout your organization or do some artificial barriers exist?

❑ Have you recently discovered internal **governance**-related policies that are impeding creativity and empowerment and limiting your ability to achieve your growth objectives?

❑ Do you find that **information** is empowering your associates to act with courage or overwhelming them to the point of analysis paralysis?

❑ Have you discovered that some of your senior associate's have reached an entitlement state, where office space and specific technologies are a status symbol, or are they focused on their assigned role and grateful for the **infrastructure** you have provided to them?

❑ Have you recently noticed that you have a tendency to provide greater **oversight** and micro-manage key initiatives, or have your associates accepted your challenge to embrace accountability and empowerment opportunities?

Your Prescription for SMART GROWTH

☐ Have you encountered recent situations where you spend more time **planning** to make plans versus focusing on executing your plans?

☐ Have you emphasized defining, implementing, and adhering to a **process** to the extreme that it is having a negative versus positive impact on your ability to support your clients?

☐ Have you had any recent occurrences as a result of a strong quarter where you have over-reacted and invested in more personnel or other business **resources** that you really could have postponed until a later date?

☐ Have you implemented too much **structure** and organizational layers in your organization that is having a detrimental impact on your ability to execute effectively?

☐ Have you recently acquired a new **technology** solution that is having a detrimental impact on your ability to support your clients?

Templates for each of these *Checklists* are available for download from http://www.SMARTGrowthSMB.com.

Epilog: Organic Growth vs. External Funding

"Stay Hungry. Stay Foolish." – Steve Jobs

The recommendations shared throughout this book were based the assumption of growing your business organically through an investment of your own passion, perspiration, creativity, convictions, values, time, and financial returns that your business generates. Of course, there are several options available to obtain funding to help you scale your business more rapidly including:

- Personal financing (i.e. credit cards)
- Unsecured or secured personal or business credit lines
- Secured personal or business credit lines
- Asset-based loans
- Family and friends
- Crowdfunding
- Small Business Administration (SBA) loans
- Accounts Receivables financing (factoring, spot-factoring)
- Angel Investors
- Venture Capital and Private Equity Firms
- Merging with a business partner or competitor
- Positioning your business to be acquired by a larger company with strong cash reserves
- Selling stock shares of your business along the lines of an Employee Stock Ownership Plan (ESOP)
- Franchising your business model
- Public Stock Offering (i.e. Initial Public Offering or IPO)

Epilog: Organic Growth vs. External Funding

While I personally believe that business owners should resist outside funding whenever possible based on my own professional experiences; there are clearly justifiable requirements that require business leaders to reach out for external financing. Some business models absolutely mandate external funding *(i.e. biotech, pharmaceutical, energy, financial institutions, manufacturing, and other businesses with substantial capital and asset requirements)*. The end result unfortunately is that outside funding quite often leads to consequences generally out of the founder's control and far too often her best interests.

I am also a strong proponent that if you need to arrange for additional external capital, you should target just enough funding, just in time to support your investment plans. In my experience there is tremendous value in a business being "hungry" and staying "hungry". Maintaining excess cash beyond your specific operational requirements and growth objectives can make your comfortable, which can result in complacency. Complacency often times decreases your sense of urgency and dulls the competitive advantages that you may hold in your market. Your senses are sharper and you pay more attention to details when your organization remains hungry. Obviously, the situation is quite different if you are a large public corporation that has been in existence for decades.

I would like to restate my conviction that *"Growth is Good"*; in fact ***"Growth is Great"*** in my mind; but it is also important to acknowledge that very serious responsibilities and accountabilities accompany growth. Business leaders face numerous new challenges when small businesses grow to mid-size businesses and mid-size businesses evolve to large corporations. Some of the challenges include adding overhead resources to deal with an increasing number of local, state, and federal regulatory and reporting requirements imposed on corporations. My experience has underscored that organic growth will most likely put you in a position to make the decisions on how long you would like to remain in the *"driver's seat"* of your business. When you introduce external capital in exchange for large equity stakes in your business; you are apt to slide over into the passenger seat or even the back seat of your business. Often times this transition occurs much sooner than anticipated.

If your primary goal for leading your business at this time is not securing an short-term financial gain *(i.e. near-term exit strategy)*, you can avoid the distractions that many public or venture-backed companies experience as they are forced to focus on quarterly financial returns and directions from a Board of Directors which may evolve to strong philosophical differences. Obviously SMB leaders cannot escape from having to worry about daily, weekly, or monthly financial results and your daily cash balance. When you are able to maintain majority ownership in your business though, it permits you to continue to maintain a laser focus on your associates and your clients, balancing the tactical demands with your strategic vision – which I find quite often to be the most successful formula to optimize your financial returns.

It is important to also emphasize that all SMB leaders should have an exit strategy, including a thoughtfully conceived succession plan for their business. Exits may be triggered by retirement, career changes, financial challenges, or an unforeseen loss of the founder or other top leaders. Conscientious business leaders should have plans in place for an organized response to the unexpected. It is an injustice to your associates and clients to not have a formal succession plan in place to ensure the on-going continuity of your business through leadership transition; smooth transition of resources and assets via a business sale to another company;

or detailed plan to dissolve your business – including an accounting for the requisite formal legal proceedings.

I welcome and encourage you to contact me if you have any questions or feedback on the recommendations I have shared throughout this book. I also invite you to contact me to discuss the specific challenges and barriers that you may be facing as you work diligently to grow your business. I can be contacted at jack <at> smartgrowthsmb.com or www.SMARTGrowthSMB.com and I am looking forward to the opportunity to speak with you.

Acknowledgements

I have had the privilege to work and learn within a diverse range of industries in a variety of executive and leadership roles throughout my professional career. I have also had the distinct honor to work with and under many business leaders who demonstrated astonishing wisdom. Many of these leaders were willing to mentor me, share their insights and experiences, and provide responses to my countless barrages of questions.

Some of the advice that I share regularly with my colleagues is (1) more often than not you do not get to choose your boss, and (2) you are more apt to learn more from your more challenging and difficult experiences than your enjoyable ones – and the corollary, you often have the opportunity to learn more from poor leaders versus exemplary leaders. I have certainly been the benefactor of both leadership extremes and have no regrets whatsoever. I have been blessed with incredible business experiences and have also had the privilege of sharing it with others through my various leadership and consulting roles.

I would like to publically note my gratitude to my colleague Chris Duke who has provided me with terrific support throughout this project. I have always greatly anticipated and enjoyed our intellectual discussions and debates on a diverse set of topics from selecting the ideal ingredients to bake the perfect cookie, creating efficient supply chains, demonstrating a business case for social media, to detailed discussions on emerging technologies to address current business challenges and opportunities.

I also would like to acknowledge the love and support from my wonderful wife Laurie who has known and supported me

Acknowledgements

throughout my entire professional career; along with my amazing daughters Lucy and Marci who continue to inspire and teach me and fill me with pride every day.

About the Author

Jack Spain has held executive and senior leadership roles in large corporations, mid-sized businesses, and small businesses for over 35 years. His professional experience includes key leadership roles in information technology, software development, marketing, business development, research, and professional services organizations. His diverse industry experience includes heavy industrial, transportation, energy, facilities and maintenance management, e-commerce, IT research and advisory services, technology commercialization, and executive recruiting.

Spain launched *Spain Technovative Solutions* and *Spain Business Advisors* in 2005 with the charter of providing business coaching and consulting services for small to mid-size businesses located in the Research Triangle Park region in central North Carolina.

He is a graduate of GE's Financial Management Program and holds a BA in Accounting and Economics from Edinboro University, has participated in executive education programs from Duke University, and has completed MBA coursework with Capella University. Spain has been a frequent speaker and presenter at industry events for several decades.

Jack published *The IT Leadership Pyramid – Essential Leadership Imperatives for Leaders of Information Technology Organizations in the 21st Century* in 2009.[46]

http://www.SMARTGrowthSMB.com
http://www.jackspain.com
http://www.linkedin.com/in/jackspain

---

[46] http://www.lulu.com/spotlight/SpainTechnovative

						6 Goals	7 Results	8 Operational Excellence	9 World Class	10 Trust	11 High Growth
1 Strategy	2 Market	3 Alignment	4 ROI	5 Technology							
12 Accountability	13 Action-orientation	14 Cash Flow	15 Client Acquisition	16 Client Service	17 Empowerment	18 Leadership	19 Listening	20 Metrics	21 Perseverance	22 Prioritization	23 Quality	24 Relationships
25 Results	26 Root cause analysis			27 Communication	28 Governance	29 Information	30 Infrastructure	31 Oversight	32 Planning	33 Process	34 Resources	35 Structure	36 Technology

www.SMARTGrowthSMB.com

Additional publications from the author include:

The IT Leadership Pyramid:
Essential Leadership Imperatives for Leaders of Information Technology Organizations in the 21ˢᵗ Century

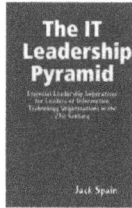

http://www.lulu.com/spotlight/SpainTechnovative